Teaching young children with autistic spectrum disorders to learn

A practical guide for parents and staff in mainstream schools and nurseries

Liz Hannah

Illustrations by Steve Lockett

THE NATIONAL
AUTISTIC SOCIETY

First published 2001 by The National Autistic Society, 393 City Road, London EC1V 1NG

ISBN 1 899280 32 4

Designed by Column Communications

Printed in Great Britain by Crowes Complete Print

Thanks to all the learning support assistants who have tried out my ideas over the years and given me such good feedback about them. Special thanks to Nikki and Marco, who make a great team, and to Ros, for the number ideas and for always being supportive.

A note from the authors

This book has been written to help parents at home and staff in mainstream schools and nurseries support and teach children aged three to seven years who have an autistic spectrum disorder. It is a practical book, pulling together some tried and tested ideas to help you and the children work and play together with success.

About the author and illustrator

Liz Hannah and Steve Lockett work for Teaching Support Services, Southwark Education Authority. Liz supports and teaches children with autistic spectrum disorders in mainstream schools and nurseries, and Steve works for the Visual Support Service.

Contents

Introduction

It is now government policy that, whenever possible, children with disabilities should have the opportunity to learn alongside their peers in mainstream schools. Thus, teachers, nursery nurses and classroom assistants are learning to meet a wide range of needs presented to them by the children they teach. Equally, parents may choose mainstream schools because they are local, so all their children go to school together, with local children, and children with disabilities of all kinds are not singled out or labelled 'different'. They become a visible, included part of their community, learning and playing alongside their peers and siblings. Indeed, it is noticeable that, especially in the early years, children with autistic spectrum disorders are attending local nurseries, playgroups and primary schools with varied amounts of extra support.

These early years are vital for all children's learning, but particularly for those with special educational needs. For children with autistic spectrum disorders, early intervention together with appropriate teaching and management will help develop crucial social, communication and play skills that provide a basis for future learning. Difficult behaviour can be reduced while the children are still young and, although this does not guarantee that there will not be difficult times, it gives them and their families a good start and helps develop confidence.

Programmes such as The National Autistic Society's EarlyBird Programme that work with parents following the diagnosis of an autistic spectrum disorder enable parents to understand the reasons for their children's difficulties. They offer practical suggestions as well as providing opportunities for sharing ideas and experiences. In nurseries, playgroups and schools, training and discussion is vital if staff are to successfully understand the complex needs of these children and help them gain new skills.

Throughout the country, local education authorities offer different choices and differing types of provision for children with autistic spectrum disorders. Some have special schools for children with complex or mixed needs, which most children attend, although children with Asperger syndrome may go into mainstream schools. Other authorities have units in mainstream schools that take children with a range of abilities in small classes with high staff-to-pupil ratios (usually one adult to every three children). These units provide some opportunities for inclusion in the mainstream schools where they are situated. However, the level of staffing in the mainstream classrooms is rarely enough to provide truly inclusive education and the children, being used to the calm, structured environment of the specialist classes, have difficulty adapting to the noisier and less structured mainstream classes when they attend them once or twice a week.

The children in the units will often have dinner and spend breaktimes with those in the mainstream classes – an arrangement needing careful management and training, not just for the adults, but also in terms of helping the children in the school understand and support the children being taught in the units. Children with autistic spectrum disorders do not learn to interact with others or learn from others simply by being placed in a playground, classroom or nursery alongside other children. They need some help in understanding what is happening, what the game is about, how they can join in, how to share, how to wait their turn. Many children with autism lack play skills and need to be taught how to play, so, although peers are important in helping teach children with autism to play, they need guidance and support to enable their input to be effective.

Resourced schools may be organised in a similar way to that of a unit but, in some authorities – particularly those that no longer have special schools – they are organised on an inclusive basis, with a high staff-to-pupil ratio (one adult to each child), including specialist teachers, nursery nurses and learning support assistants. The children are placed in their mainstream class where they follow the National Curriculum, differentiated to meet their needs. When they need individual help or are having difficulty coping in the classroom, small group or individual teaching and relaxation is provided. A high level of expertise develops in resourced schools because all the adults in the school are involved in teaching and supporting children with autistic spectrum disorders.

Many young children with an autistic spectrum disorder go to their local nursery or playgroup. If they have a Statement of Special Educational Needs, they may have been allocated a number of hours support from a learning support assistant. Input from a peripatetic teacher and speech and language therapist with experience and knowledge of autistic spectrum disorders can be vital at this time in order to maximise the benefit of nursery education to the child. They should provide targets and strategies and model some of the teaching methods described in this book. If such back-up is not available – and in some areas this will be the case – there are training courses all over the country providing help and information, as well as some excellent books (see the References and Further reading sections at the back of the book).

Playgroups and nurseries encourage children to learn and develop through communication, play and social interaction – all areas in which a child with an autistic spectrum disorder has difficulties. Some of the strategies that are known to help children with autism may seem contrary to the whole meaning of inclusion, and structured teaching is a particular example of this. However, a balance should be reached where the child's needs are met across all areas of development. If structured teaching reduces anxiety, helping the child learn new skills that can be practised and developed in a group situation, then it has a positive outcome, supporting inclusion.

Many of the strategies given in this book assume that adult help is available to support the child, whether at pre-school, nursery or school. If there are no extra resources, many of the ideas suggested only take a few minutes and can be used throughout the day as opportunities arise. The important first stage is to have a good individual education plan based on an assessment of the child's abilities and using small steps to achieve progress. Some examples of individual education plans are included and show short-term targets that can be achieved in a few weeks. If targets are too difficult, it is easy to lose confidence and give up because children with autism can be so determined to follow their own agenda. Do not give up! You may need to break things down into smaller steps or look at your strategies for more creative ideas, but keep going.

Working with children with autistic spectrum disorders can be very rewarding and exciting. Try to find support by, for example, meeting up sometimes with others doing similar work, using the internet to find articles, advice and strategies and working closely in a team with colleagues and other professionals.

A word to parents

Although many activities in this book are school-based, much of what is suggested, particularly in the early sections, has also been written for you. You know your child best – the way he thinks and the things that motivate him. Supporting your child's learning at home and understanding how he learns can be a positive experience for both of you.

Note

Four out of five children diagnosed with autistic spectrum disorders are boys. For this reason and to avoid long, convoluted sentences, throughout the book I have used 'he' when referring to a child and 'she' for a parent or teacher. However, all the information in the book applies to both sexes.

The terms 'autistic spectrum disorder' and 'autism' are used synonymously.

The needs of children
with autistic spectrum
disorders

The needs of children with autistic spectrum disorders

'Autistic spectrum disorders' is a broad term that includes autism and Asperger syndrome, pervasive developmental disorder, pathological demand avoidance syndrome and semantic pragmatic disorder. It is a broad spectrum of need and includes children with varying degrees of difficulties and varying areas of ability.

Areas of difficulty

The difficulties children have are in three main areas, called the 'triad of impairments':

- communication
- social interaction
- imagination

Difficulties in the area of communication may include:

- a lack of desire to communicate at all
- communicating needs only
- disordered or delayed language
- poor non-verbal communication, including eye contact, gesture, expression, body language
- good language, but with no social awareness – unable to start or keep up a conversation, only talking about own interests, failing to listen to others, assuming other people know what they are thinking and so on
- pedantic language that is very literal and shows poor or no understanding of idioms and jokes.

Regarding social awareness and interaction, children may have the following kinds of difficulty:

- no desire to interact with others
- being interested in others in order to have their needs met
- possibly being affectionate but on their own terms and not always at the right time or place
- lack of motivation to please others
- friendly but with odd interactions
- no understanding of unspoken social rules
- limited interaction, particularly with unfamiliar people or in unfamiliar circumstances.

Difficulties with lack of imagination and rigidity of thought may include the following:

- using toys as objects – for example, fiddling with the wheels on a car rather than pushing it along the ground

The needs of children
with autistic spectrum
disorders

- an inability to play or write imaginatively
- resisting change – for example, crying hysterically if taken to school by a different route or becoming upset if something is arranged differently
- playing the same game over and over – sometimes based on a video or television character – but unwilling to follow others' ideas
- learning things easily by rote but with no understanding
- an inability to see things from other people's points of view
- following rules rigidly and not understanding exceptions
- limited ability to predict what will happen next or to recall/reuse past experiences without visual object cues.

Other difficulties found in children with autistic spectrum disorders include:

- sensory difficulties – many children have a heightened awareness of different sounds, colours, textures and tastes that can cause them extreme discomfort, so they are often sensitive to sounds that are found daily in the classroom, like chairs scraping on the floor, and they may be troubled by sounds, colours, textures and smells that are not noticed by others
- sleeping difficulties – once they have a certain routine it is very difficult to change it
- eating difficulties – they may be sensitive to certain textures, will not try new things and so on
- difficulties developing independence skills
- obsessions or insistence on certain rituals
- fears and phobias that can include everyday things such as certain advertisements, pictures in books, specific songs, young children crying
- poor fine motor skills
- poor spatial awareness
- focusing on minor details and ignoring the main picture – for example, looking at a spot of dirt on the floor when they are in the middle of a chasing game
- no sense of their own or other's safety, which makes them very vulnerable
- children with Asperger syndrome are often clumsy and may have dyspraxia.

How difficulties affect children at school

The areas of difficulty the children experience may result in:

- a lack of understanding of what is being said
- an understanding of some words but not the more complex meanings behind them
- poor listening and attention skills
- frequent distraction from the purpose of the activity
- a determination to do what they want to do and not what they are asked to do
- an inability to share, always wanting things their way
- the inability to play or understand the rules of games
- learning by rote with no understanding of what has been learned
- a lack of awareness of others and how they may be affected by their actions – for example, stepping on other children without noticing, closing doors in people's faces, upsetting other's games

The needs of children
with autistic spectrum
disorders

- showing anxiety by developing behaviour that is difficult to manage
- insisting that rules are followed rigidly or that things are done in certain ways
- calling out in class or assembly
- having no concern for others – for example, not understanding why it is bad to throw sand
- having obsessive topics of conversation and talking at people rather than with them
- developing dependence on particular adults or routines
- having difficulty generalising skills they have learnt to other situations
- insisting on being at the front or back of the line or sitting in a certain place on the carpet
- showing distress if an error is made by them or someone else
- having difficulty making choices
- having difficulty talking about something that has happened in the past or putting themselves in an imaginary situation.

The key to making progress

Every child is different and has different degrees of need. The list above has been written to raise awareness of the difficulties a child with autism may have that will affect the way he learns and behaves.

The key to offering good support and enabling progress where possible is to understand the individual child – no two children with autistic spectrum disorders will be the same.

The needs of children
with autistic spectrum
disorders

Chapter 1

Developing early communication

From a very young age, babies have been shown to imitate facial expressions and sounds made by their caregivers. For the first six months of life, parents respond to many of their baby's sounds and movements as though they have meaning: reinforcing and building up a dialogue of turn-taking and interaction using noises, movement, eye contact, facial expression and 'social timing'.

Goldbart, 1988

Children with autistic spectrum disorders have difficulty in these important areas of non-verbal communication. They may avoid eye contact and be extremely active or placid and self-absorbed. They do not point to draw attention to things and share their interest with others. They have difficulty imitating sounds and gestures and attaching meaning to them.

Early communication skills overlap with social interaction skills and play. These, taken together, make a good starting point as the skills involved will build a foundation for intervention across the triad of impairments found in autism. As you will recall, these are difficulties in communication, social interaction and lack of imagination with inflexibility of thought.

The following pages include activities to develop the earliest social, communication and play skills under the following headings:

- Learning to play: building a relationship
- Interactive play
- Strategies to encourage eye contact
- Turn-taking activities to help develop early communication
- Awareness of tongue and mouth
- Developing breath control
- Using music to develop communication skills
- Making choices
- Adapting the environment to encourage communication
- Developing language
- Using signs and symbols.

Learning to play: building a relationship

Most young children with autistic spectrum disorders have limited interests that are often repetitive and solitary. They may resist an adult or child joining in their play. Cuddles and games will usually be on their terms.

The first step when teaching a child new skills is to build a relationship where the child

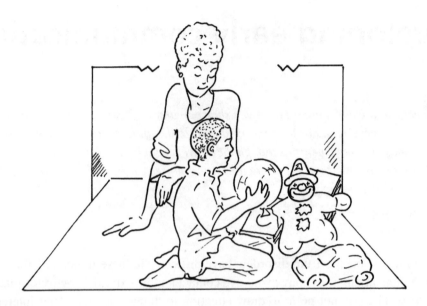

enjoys being with you and will join in things you want to do. It is important not to be deterred by the verbal or non-verbal 'leave me alone' message the child may be giving.

What you can do

Begin by sitting beside the child, watching him play. He may get up and walk away every time you go to sit next to him, so it helps if you have a very motivating toy with you – for example, bubbles, a squeaking toy, spinning top, music.

When the child accepts your presence, comment on what he is doing in a positive way. If he is looking at a book you could say, 'That's a big book. It looks good. Turn the page. Finished!'

With a young child, you may want to sing about what he is doing. For example, to the tune of *Frère Jacques* you could sing 'John is jumping, John is jumping, yes he is, yes he is, jumping, jumping, jumping, jumping, jumping, jumping, jumping John, jumping John.'

Gradually join in with what the child is doing. At first, just copy what he does. With some children it may be necessary to sit alongside. If the child is looking at a book but does not want to share it with you, you could sit alongside and say, 'I'm reading too!' Some

children will allow you to share their book but you will have to look at the pages they have chosen. That is fine because what you want to do is let the child become used to you sharing their space without becoming a threat.

If the child is playing outside with a ball or hoop but will not let you play with it too, find a similar ball or hoop and copy what he does. If he likes to run up and down, run up and down beside him or race up and down holding hands.

When the child accepts you alongside copying his actions, start to take the lead sometimes. If he always does the same thing, change it a little. Make new suggestions seem really exciting. For example, if you have been watching a music video together, start gently moving to the rhythm of the music. If you have been running up and down together, change direction and go round in circles.

When the child starts to follow your lead sometimes and allows you to follow his lead sometimes, you have the start of a good relationship. Keep it up! Be enthusiastic, be exciting, be active. Use some of the play ideas on the following pages or make up ideas of your own. Simple things are usually the most appealing to young children.

Interactive play

Interactive play is any play that involves two or more participants anticipating and developing their actions in relation to each other. It develops early social interaction and play skills but is also a form of communication as each participant in the game builds on the other's actions, extending, changing, keeping going, slowing down, speeding up.

It is an important starting point to help children with autistic spectrum disorders acknowledge the importance of others and develop early social and play skills. It may feel easier to play with babies and toddlers in this way but it can usefully be developed to help older children with autistic spectrum disorders who have difficulty interacting with adults or peers.

Rough and tumble

This is the name given to games that involve vigorous activity and excitement. An adult will pick a baby up and toss him in the air. The baby will scream with excitement and lift his hands up for more. The adult does it again and the baby laughs and looks at the adult, moving his body up and down to show he wants the action repeated. 'Again?' the adult asks and the baby laughs with glee in anticipation of another exciting ride through the air.

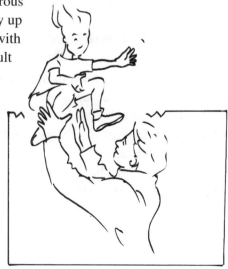

Many types of game come into this category. You want the child to enjoy himself enough to show that he wants you to do it again. You want him to move his body, pull you, look at your face, laugh in anticipation, make a sound or ask for more. At first you may need to prompt him. Say 'You want more?' and wait for a response. It may be a subtle flicker of the eye or a less subtle thump, but you know what it means. 'You want more!' you say and repeat the game. As the child develops his communication skills, you make it harder for him to get the desired response by moving through some of the following stages:

- a slight movement
- a definite movement
- fleeting eye contact
- a definite look
- a sign or gesture showing what he wants
- a symbol
- a sound
- a word – 'bubbles!' or 'tickle!' for example
- a phrase – 'more tickles' – followed by a sentence – 'chase me again!'

Note that rough and tumble play is a very physical type of play. Many mainstream nurseries and schools now discourage children being touched by adults during play. This is an issue that should be discussed and included in special educational needs policies by nurseries and schools so that staff have clear guidelines of what is acceptable and safe.

In thinking about these issues, it can be helpful for mainstream schools to look at the guidelines followed in special school settings. It is important to remember that children who have any kind of sensory difficulty may be at a very early stage of their sensory development and need much more physical interaction with the adults around them than other children.

Rough and tumble play has to be enjoyable to the child or the purpose is lost. Introduce different ideas gradually to see what the child really likes. Some children dislike being touched and it is important to respect this and find other ways of developing interactive play. If you are in a mainstream setting, it may be possible to use facilities like soft play and large physio balls in resource bases or special schools. Some rough and tumble play is more suited to being enjoyed at home with very small children and thought should be given to whether or not it is safe to lift and swing older children at school.

Types of rough and tumble play
- Throw the child in the air and catch him.
- Give the child a ride on your back or legs.
- Play with soft play equipment – bouncing, jumping, climbing, rolling.
- Push the child gently in to a ball pool or on to a soft mat.
- Bounce or roll on a big ball.
- Play tickling games or blow raspberries on ticklish places.

- Spin the child round while holding their hands or waist.
- Play monsters or 'I'm coming to get you!' games.
- Swing or catch the child on a large piece of fabric.
- Play hide and seek or peep-o under a rug or around doorways, windows and hiding spaces.
- Play jump and fall down games on thick PE mats, old sofas or any soft surface.

Repetitive phrases, singing and rhymes are often an important part of interactive play. They help the child anticipate what is going to happen and build up the level of excitement. When swinging a young child round, you might say, 'a one … a two … a threeeeee!' or, when playing chasing games, 'I'm coming to get you … here I come!' creeping up and then, when the child looks expectantly, racing forward to catch them in your arms.

Two rhymes for swinging a child on a piece of fabric

You need a good-sized rug, blanket or piece of strong fabric, two strong adults and a child. Swing to the rhythm of the rhyme and keep swinging all the way through until the last line. Then, tip the child out or drop him carefully on to a soft mat.

Bacon and eggs

One o'clock, still in bed	Five o'clock, still in bed
Two o'clock, still in bed	Six o'clock, still in bed
Three o'clock, still in bed	Seven o'clock, still in bed
Four o'clock, still in bed	Eight o'clock, bacon and eggs!

For the second rhyme, sing the words below to the tune of *The Drunken Sailor*, swinging the blanket throughout.

Hooray and up he rises!

What shall we do with [sing child's name]? (Repeat three times.)
Early in the morning?
Hooray and up he rises (Repeat three times, lifting the blanket up on 'up')
Early in the morning. (Swing, then say one, two, three and tip the child out, carefully, as before.)

Three tickling rhymes

Check first that the child concerned likes to be tickled.

Bumble bee

Bumble bee, bumble bee,

buzzy, buzzy bumble bee (walk your fingers up the child's arm or body)

bumble bee, bumble bee... (pause for anticipation)

buzzy, buzzy, bumble bee! (tickle him under the chin, arm or wherever he enjoys being tickled.)

I'm coming to tickle your tummy

I'm coming to tickle your tummy, (with tickling fingers wriggling, gradually move closer to the child's tummy)

I'm coming to tickle your tummy

I'm coming to tickle your tummy... (pause to create sense of anticipation)

Tickertickertickerticker (tickle tummy).

This little fish

This little fish (wriggle your forefinger)

hid behind a rock (hide your finger)

came creeping out... (make your wriggling finger slowly creep out)

and gave you a shock! (your finger jumps up and tickles the child)

Other ideas for interactive play

Water play

As well as pouring water out of or in to containers of different sizes and shapes, try the following ideas. They can be used to capture a child's interest and develop joint attention – that is, adult and child sharing enjoyment and interest in the activity.

- Colour the water.
- Froth up baby bubble bath with a whisk and blow it or make shapes in it.
- Build a tower of blocks on a bridge across the water and anticipate the splash as they fall in!
- Pierce a plastic bottle in a pattern on the sides and bottom so the sand or water pours out from unexpected places. Use a different bottle every day with a different pattern.

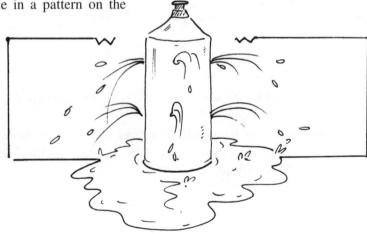

- Blow bubbles with a straw in a cup containing a little bit of washing-up liquid and some bubble bath. Lovely bubbles, lovely sound.
- Blow up a balloon and float it in the water.
- Push it under and let it go so the air bubbles out. Try metallic balloons for variety and durability.
- Use wind-up toys in the water, especially noisy ones, such as frogs, ducks, boats.
- Put cobblestones, driftwood, seaweed, shells and so on in the water and use them to create movement.

Play with puppets

The most interesting puppets are hand puppets that make a noise. If you do not have a noisy puppet, using strong thread, sew a squeaker inside one or attach bells to the outside. Unusual puppets with bright colours, large beaks, long legs and furry textures are popular but a very simple puppet with a squeak will attract most young children.

Introduce the puppet slowly as the child may be afraid of it initially. Use it to tickle, talk, dance, sing and make funny noises. Encourage the child to try it on his hand. Take turns or use two puppets to have a conversation.

Puppets are good at the beginning and end of a play session to sing 'hello' and 'goodbye' songs. They often draw the child's attention to you and provide a good opening for other play activities. Puppets also encourage taking turns and social interaction – skills that are discussed in subsequent chapters.

Outdoor play

Push the child on a swing. Ask if he wants more pushes. If possible, push him from the front so that you can see the expression on his face and respond to it.

Jump on a trampoline. If it is big enough, jump together; if not, stand on the side and help the child jump or jump along with him. Stop and ask the child if he wants to jump some more and wait for a response before starting again.

Play chase or hide and seek. Playing in a tunnel can be fun or hiding behind a tree or an adult's legs. This is an outdoor version of peep-o and can be very exciting.

When children will not play

It can be hard to engage some children with autistic spectrum disorders in interactive play. If you have been through the suggestions above and still have difficulty encouraging a child to play, try the following ideas.

Collect motivating toys and objects

These could include spinning tops that play a tune, furry animals that make a sound when hit, balls that light up when bounced, helicopters that fly up when you pull a trigger, torches with coloured lenses, a tape recorder with a tape of a favourite piece of music, a Disney character from a favourite video, a piece of fabric covered in sequins, a helter skelter, a piece of string.

Talk to all the adults who know the child. Somewhere in these conversations you will find something the child enjoys that can be the beginning of a game.

Let the child lead

Try to have two identical toys and copy what the child does with his. If the child likes playing in water, you play in water too. Do not be put off when the child walks away from you – try again later. If he likes lying on his back gazing at the sky, then try it yourself! You will find some of these seemingly pointless activities enjoyable and can share that enjoyment in companionable silence.

If you reach a point where you are happy together, move things along a little. Add a variation. If you are looking at the sky, try looking at it through red glasses or a red piece of fabric. Bring some bubbles and blow them into the air. Have another person draw around your shapes with chalk as you lie there. Reach out and hold hands or roll across the ground.

Develop the child's interest

Some children love string and so on. If so, collect different-coloured ribbons, glittery string and pieces of rope. Tie a bell, pompom or balloon on the end, make a snake with some cotton reels, make puppets with string for their hair. If he obsessively wants to unravel the string or chew it, you will have to judge when and how much string to allow. Changing an obsession into creative play can be difficult but it can provide an important way into a child's world.

Making time for play

As well as grasping opportunities throughout the day to develop play and communication skills, it can be helpful to set aside a specific time each day when you take the child out of the classroom or nursery for some interactive play.

Include the play time as part of the child's daily routine, consistently signalled by a symbol, object or word. Keep some notes so that everyone knows what you have done and what responses you may be able to work on at other times. You may find it best at these times to play in an area where there are no other distractions and keep to a small number of activities.

Playmates

Although interactive play initially builds on the relationship between adult and child, at a later stage it can be helpful to include one or two other children. They can act as positive role models, showing enjoyment in interactive play activities.

Strategies to encourage eye contact

Eye contact is a natural communication skill and it can feel difficult to talk to someone if they are not looking at you. If you are teaching a child a new skill, you want to know he is paying attention to what you are saying and doing. Teaching him to look at you is an important part of gaining his attention.

Eye contact is a non-verbal skill that many children with autistic spectrum disorders do not develop naturally. In fact, children with autism may feel uncomfortable looking directly at you or not understand how hard they are supposed to look, so care should be taken to build the skill gradually and not to make too big an issue of it.

What you can do

To encourage the development of eye contact, you will need anything that might gain the child's attention and reward him for looking. You could use, for example, bubbles, balloons, puppets with bells, noisy, bright or shiny toys, cause and effect toys with switches and buttons, food or, indeed, any other items the child particularly likes.

You can work on eye contact any time when there are not too many distractions, at home, nursery or school. Make the exercises fun by using motivating toys and rewards and praise a good response by saying 'good looking' while giving the child the reward. If he steadfastly refuses to look at you, reward a near look and keep working on it, always rewarding the best response.

Give the child enough time to respond but do not wait so long that he loses interest in the activity or becomes frustrated and starts to cry. Timing is important – it is better to accept a near response and say 'Good try' than lose the opportunity all together.

At first, praise and reward the most fleeting eye contact as it will not be intentional. When the child begins to understand that you want him to look at you, increase your expectation before giving the reward. However, it is important not to teach the child to stare at you; try to keep it natural.

Hold an interesting toy or piece of food near your face. For instance, you may have a puppet with bells on that the child wants. Shake it near your face, saying, 'You want the puppet?' and give it to him when he looks at you. Blowing bubbles is another good activity as the child will be looking at your face. Hold the wand near your face and say, 'You want bubbles?' and wait for the look before blowing.

Other good activities for developing eye contact

- Play peep-o behind anything – a sheet, towel, your hands, a cupboard door, the end of a tunnel.
- Use a big mirror to play dressing-up games, pull funny faces or put on face paint. Say 'Look at me!' and make an action or gesture when the child looks at you in the mirror – put on a big hat, make a funny noise, blow a kiss.

- Play *Row, row, row your boat* or other games or tickling games where the child is facing you. Ask if he wants 'more' but only repeat it if he looks towards you or at you. Play chasing or spinning games but only chase or spin him when he looks at you.
- When you want to gain the child's attention – for example, if you are sitting down to do some work – say 'look at the book' and make sure you have his attention before beginning.

Turn-taking activities to help develop early communication

Turn-taking activities help build a social dialogue between a child and an adult, then between a child and his peers.

What you can do

To begin with, activities should be simple and very motivating for the child. It is important to remember that children with learning difficulties may take longer to respond than you expect, so give them plenty of time before prompting a response. You will be surprised how frequently a child takes his turn just as you are about to do it for him.

When playing turn-taking games it can be helpful to say, 'My turn, your turn' or 'Mummy's turn, George's turn', so the child learns to associate the words with the idea of waiting his turn. Then, when another child joins in, you can start to add to the list – for example, 'Molly's turn, George's turn, Johnny's turn' – thus building in the more complex social skill of sharing with a friend. An object or symbol can be used to show whose turn it is.

Many play activities can be shared in a turn-taking game. Here are a few ideas, starting with very simple games.

- Take turns spinning a top or pressing a switch on a cause and effect toy (one that does something exciting when you touch it in some way, such as a music box, a toy that spins, toys that make noises when they are banged or pushed, toys that are operated with switches, pop-up toys).
- Take turns dropping balls down a tube or down a helter skelter.
- Take turns blowing bubbles, blowing a paper windmill, pouring water or sand.
- Take turns rolling a car down a ramp.
- Take turns laying a brick to build a tower or knocking the tower over.
- Take turns playing peep-o with a scarf or piece of fabric.
- Take turns dropping shapes into a posting box.
- Take turns banging a drum.
- Take turns bouncing a rubber ball.

More interactive turn-taking activities involve the child acknowledging your part in a game and playing with you. This can be more difficult, so it is easiest if at first you work on this in a small space with no distractions. You may need another adult to show the child what he has to do. Try some of the following ideas.

- Push a car to the child and wait for him to push it back to you.

- Roll, throw or kick a ball and wait for the child to return it to you – start with rolling, which is best done sitting on the floor with your legs out so there is a clear area in which to play.
- Bounce or roll a ball in a blanket or towel by holding the ends of the fabric.
- Hit a balloon back and forth between you.
- Blow a balloon up and take turns to let it go, in the air or some water.
- Take turns to draw around each other's hands or feet.

- Have a pretend conversation on the telephone, taking turns to speak.
- Take turns to pour and drink a pretend cup of tea.

When you want another child to join in, you can try the ideas given below, first with an adult, then with a child or a small group of two or three.

- Take turns to turn pages and lift the flap of a book.
- Take turns to go down a slide.
- Take turns to squirt a balloon or target with water or paint.
- Play simple games of lotto, taking turns to pick up a card.
- Do a puzzle together, taking turns to place each piece.
- Dip a tennis ball or marble in paint and take turns to roll it on a piece of paper.
- Take turns to hold, stroke or feed a pet.
- Take turns to use an implement – for example, a rolling pin to roll dough, a biscuit cutter, the mouse when using the computer.
- Take turns in a singing game where one child sits in the middle.

Turn-taking songs
Here are three good turn-taking songs to try with a small group.

Johnny's in the Garden (Chant the words with lots of expression!)
You will need a fan or piece of card, a water sprayer and some talcum powder.
'Johnny' sits in the middle while the others watch and join in the words if they can.

> Johnny's in the garden (sitting on a chair)
> Blow, wind, blow (make some wind with the fan or card)
> Plip-plop raindrops (spray with water)
> And down comes the snow (lightly scatter talcum powder).

The next child then takes his turn.

Jack in the Box
Sing this to the tune of *Here we go round the mulberry bush*.
You will need a large box stable enough for the child to sit on.

> Jack in the box jumps *up* out of bed (child jumps up from box)
> He makes me laugh when he wobbles his head (child wobbles his head)
> I gently push him down again (the other children push the child down)
> But Jack in the Box jumps *up* instead (child jumps up again).

The Hokey-Cokey
One child goes in the middle of the circle while the others stand in a circle around him.

> Put Joseph in, put Joseph out (lead the child in and out of the circle)
> In, out, in, out
> And tickle him all about (tickle or shake him)
> You do the Hokey-Cokey and turn around (wriggle hips and turn around)
> That's what it's all about.

Awareness of tongue and mouth

Some non-verbal children may not be aware of their tongue and lips and what they can do, although they are very important for forming sounds. Exercises that help to encourage oral awareness and movement of the tongue include the following:

- sticking your tongue out and asking the child to copy you: develop this when he can stick his tongue out in imitation by asking him to imitate you moving your tongue up and down and from side to side around your mouth
- putting honey or jam on the child's lips and round his mouth so that he will lick it off with his tongue
- blowing out your cheeks and see if the child can copy you
- blowing raspberries with your lips and ask the child to try and copy you
- doing an 'Indian howl'
- blowing kisses
- putting lipstick on and make kisses on a mirror
- licking a lollipop or pretend to lick an ice-cream.

Developing breath control

Breath control is also important for developing and controlling sounds. Exercises you can use to develop breath control include:

- blowing bubbles with a bubble wand or through a straw
- blowing or sucking through a straw
- blowing a whistle or kazoo
- blowing dandelion clocks
- blowing boats on the water
- blowing frothed up bubble bath off their or your hands
- blowing feathers
- blowing on a mirror or window and making a pattern
- blowing candles
- blowing paper windmills to make them spin.

Using music to develop communication skills

Most young children love music and sometimes their language first begins to emerge as the words of a song. Singing can make unpleasant tasks more enjoyable, help develop play, soothe and give pleasure.

If you do not know many simple children's songs, it is possible to buy or borrow from the library suitable tapes and videos, often with a book giving the words and actions. Short, repetitive songs are best, so the child learns phrases, learns to anticipate a word or action and wants to fill in the gaps at the appropriate places.

What you can do

Try making up songs to describe your actions or those of the child. A 'singing commentary' about a child's play can be a good way to join in, comment and develop a turn-taking dialogue. Copy the child's actions sometimes, then change the sound a little bit and see if he will copy you.

Sing a song with actions – for example, where the child gets a tickle. When the song is familiar, leave a gap before the action to see if the child will ask for the tickle or make a movement to show anticipation. Make sure the gap is long enough to give the child plenty of time to respond, but not so long that he loses interest in the tickle.

Sit facing the child or have the child facing you on your lap. Sing simple nursery songs and, when they are familiar, leave out key words or phrases to encourage the child to fill in the spaces. Make a big thing of this, leave a gap, look expectantly at the child, give him enough time to respond but not so long that you lose the rhythm of the song completely. Do not give up if the child does not respond – keep up the expectation that he will fill in the gap with a sound or gesture. It often happens when you are not expecting it.

A good song for copying a sound, action or word is *Row, row, row your boat,* the words to which follow.

Row, row, row your boat
  Row, row, row your boat, gently down the stream (have the child facing you, hold hands and row back and forth)
  If you see a crocodile, don't forget to scream AHHHHH! (scream!)

  Row, row, row your boat, gently down the river,
  If you see a polar bear, don't forget to shiver. BRRRRR! (hold your arms across your body)

  Row, row, row your boat, gently round the lake
  If you hear a hissing noise it's probably a snake (SSSSSSS!) (make a loud hissing sound)

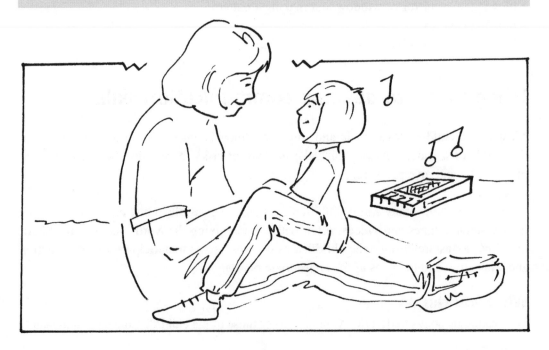

Sometimes children will only sing on their own, stopping when you join in. Do not worry about this. Try to join in gradually, singing along to the last line or very quietly.

You could also try taping your child while he is singing and playing it back to him. This helps him to develop an awareness of his voice and what it can do. Children usually enjoy hearing themselves on tape, although they may be confused at first.

Songs can be a good way to teach imitation skills. Say you have a sound or an action and want the child to copy you. First, show him what to do and prompt him if necessary. Then, withdraw the prompt and see if he will copy the action by himself.

You can also use simple actions, such as clapping, or drums or shakers and get the child to copy your action with that. This then becomes a good turn-taking activity.

Here are two good songs for developing imitation and turn-taking skills.

> *Johnny can you do this?*
> Johnny can you do this, do this, do this (use the child's name in place of 'Johnny')
> Johnny can you do this
> Just like me.
>
> Johnny can you clap your hands, clap your hands, clap your hands, (your turn)
> Johnny can you clap your hands,
> Just like me.
> Clapping, clapping, clapping, clapping, clapping, (child's turn)
> Clapping, clapping, clapping,
> Just like me.
>
> Johnny can you bang the drum, bang the drum, bang the drum, (your turn)
> Johnny can you bang the drum
> Just like me.
> Banging, banging, banging, banging, banging, (child's turn)
> banging, banging, banging
> Just like me.

> *Put your hand on your head*
> (Sing this to the tune of *If you're happy and you know it*).
> Put your hand on your head, on your head,
> Put your hand on your head, on your head,
> Put your hand on your head, put your hand on your head,
> Put your hand on your head, on your head.
>
> Put your hand on your nose, on your nose ...
>
> Put your hand on your tummy, on your tummy ... (and so on)

These and similar songs can also be used to help teach body parts and body awareness. There are a couple of other strategies that are very worthwhile too. Relaxation tapes, for example, are useful to help you relax with a child and spend some gentle time together. Start with a short time and always use the same music, so the child knows it is time to relax. Lie in a comfortable place – preferably a darkened room or quiet area – and let the music wash over you. A specific cushion or blanket can be used to show the child it is time for relaxation.

Some children love certain songs from favourite videos or songs they have heard on the radio. These are very useful to have on tape as a reward or for times when you want the child to be calm – for example, in the car.

Making choices

Offering choices to children is a good way to help them learn how useful communication skills can be. This also helps give them a sense of purpose, of having some control over their environment.

You may need to start by offering a favourite item and something you know the child does not like. However, as soon as he has grasped the idea of choosing, you can offer two favourite items to choose from. If you are asking the child to make a choice between snacks, for example, hold them up and say clearly, 'You want a *biscuit* or *crisps*?', emphasising the words as you do so. If he always chooses biscuits to have for his snack, but you know he likes apples and bananas, try taking the biscuits away altogether and offering a choice between the two types of fruit. This may cause difficulties at first if the child is used to having biscuits, but, after a several days, he may be able to cope well with choosing alternatives and accepting them happily.

There are many opportunities throughout the day to offer choices. At first, do not offer more than two choices at once, as this could be confusing, but make the choices meaningful. If a child at home always chooses the video he wants, put them away out of sight and just offer a choice of two. The child may grab both the videos, but you can prompt him to point to or take the one he wants. If he still grabs at both the videos simultaneously, keep them at different distances apart and give the first one he touches. He will soon understand that he has to choose the one he prefers.

When the child understands that pictures can be used to represent real objects, you can also use pictorial choice boards. For example, make up cards with copies of pictures from the covers of the videos and teach the child to choose by pointing to the appropriate card or taking the card and handing it to you (see the section on the Picture Exchange Communication System and using symbols, page 37). Symbols, drawings, photographs and copies of packaging can all be used to make choice boards but do not clutter them with too many choices at first. If the child always makes the same choice, leave that picture card out sometimes or put a cross over it to show that it is not available.

Good times to offer choices

Start by holding up two cards, then increase the number of choices.

- Choose between toys, videos, books or tapes. For example, 'You want the *animal* book or the *monster* book?' When the child reaches for a book, 'You want the *monster* book. OK, we'll have the *monster* book'. Then put the other book away.
- Choose between snacks and drinks or choose a filling for a sandwich.
- Choose between songs and games. You can have a picture for each song and put them on a board so the child can choose the one he wants.
- Choose items of clothing – for example, plain socks or patterned socks.
- Choose an outing – feed the ducks or have a go on the swings.
- Choose colours for colouring, beads for threading or wooden building blocks. For example, 'You want the *red* pen or the *blue* pen?' or 'You want the *round* bead or the *square* bead?' or 'You want a *big* block or a *little* block?'

Adapting the environment to encourage communication

In most homes and nurseries, children's toys and activities are not placed on high shelves or in locked cupboards. They are readily accessible so that children can learn by exploring. However, for young children with severe communication difficulties, providing easy access to everything they need removes important opportunities to teach them to communicate with others and show how rewarding such communication can be.

Adapting the environment to provide more opportunities for communication to occur needs to be planned carefully. You do not want to make things more difficult by putting favourite toys in tantalising view but on a high shelf, resulting in the child making a dangerous climb to reach it. Similarly, in a nursery, there may be little you can do to change the general environment. However, even given these kinds of constraints, there are many little things you can do throughout the day to help develop communication skills.

Children with autistic spectrum disorders may ask for what they want by eye pointing, pointing, dragging you towards the object, standing under or beside the cupboard or shelf where things are kept, crying, speaking aloud (but not always asking somebody) or having a tantrum. Consider how the child communicates his needs and try to move him on to the next stage by teaching pointing and the use of eye contact or by using symbols, pictures, sounds or spoken words.

What you can do

When you first try the ideas that follow, the child may be perplexed and become frustrated very quickly. However, if you model the correct response before he becomes upset, he will soon begin to understand what is expected and some of the things you try will become little jokes between you.

- Keep favourite toys and food in a locked cupboard. Stick symbols, photographs or pictures on the cupboard using Velcro and teach the child to bring you the picture of the thing he wants. This can work well for videos, snacks and favourite toys. If you do not want a child to have a particular toy or snack, you can remove the card or place a red cross over it.

- If a child is able to ask for what he wants but seldom does so, symbols and picture cards will help him understand that he has to go to an adult and ask for them. You can then encourage him to use a word, phrase or sentence to do this, depending on his language ability. You should always emphasise what the child has said – for example, if he says 'book', you reply, 'You want the *book*. Let's get the book.'

- You can set up situations where you 'forget' to give the child something important, like giving a cup for a drink but not putting any drink in it or not giving a spoon at dinner-time when you know he has his favourite dessert and will need a spoon to eat it. Sometimes you may have to prompt a request if the child cries or sits silently but give plenty of time for him to ask for himself. A communication book or board that contains pictures, symbols or written words (if the child can read) can be a very useful prompt for a reluctant speaker.

- You can also try giving something that is wrong – a pencil with a broken point or a plastic biscuit instead of a real one, for example – or do something wrong – such as trying to put a sock on a hand instead of a foot. Whatever you do, make sure that you give enough time for the child to respond and try to choose things that are motivating for him.

- When you are playing a game or doing a favourite puzzle, keep a piece in your hand and see if the child responds by asking for it.

- When you give the child something he wants, do not give it all at once. If you have crisps, keep the packet and hand them one at a time as he requests them. Similarly, if you have balls for a helter skelter, dolls in a doll's house or pieces for a posting box, keep them and wait until the child asks for the next one. The request may be in the form of a look, gesture, symbol, word or sentence – whatever level of communication you are working towards. You may also need to teach 'no' so the child is able to tell you he does not want any of the choices available. A symbol with a red cross, a sign or the word 'no' can be taught as appropriate to the individual child.

See also page 37 about the Picture Exchange Communication System.

Developing language

Some health authorities provide excellent speech and language therapy support. These professionals will assess each child's needs and provide suitable activities and strategies to help language development. In general, language strategies are aimed at developing functional language, which means that children are helped to develop language skills in the classroom or at home while doing activities that are part of their daily routine. This includes play, daily routines such as mealtimes, storytime, bathtime and varied activities like trips out, cooking, singing or artwork. In fact, most things that children do throughout their day can become opportunities to develop their language with a little adult support.

The ideas given below offer some ideas for how to help develop language while doing other activities.

What you can do

Working with children with minimal vocabulary
The following are some ideas for how to work with young children who are vocalising but have minimal vocabulary.

- Use language clearly in a happy voice. People speak to babies in a sing-song voice and this is helpful to all children who are developing language. It helps make your message clear if your voice is expressive and you sound interesting. You should always stress the main words.
- Sing familiar songs and rhymes and leave a gap before the last word or phrase to see if the child will anticipate by making a sound or say the word. For example, you could sing 'The wheels on the bus go round and round, round and round, round and round, the wheels on the bus go round and round, all day long.' With this song, you can leave out the last word of a line or the last phrase, 'all day long', which remains the same throughout all the verses in the song.
- When looking at books with a child who is still at an early stage of language development, choose picture books. You can point to the pictures and use words as labels.
- There are some wonderful storybooks for young children that have repetitive phrases on each page. When the child knows the story, leave out the last word or phrase and see if he will say it. Do not forget to show anticipation in your voice and wait for several seconds so that the child has time to respond.
- Play games where you are using the same word or phrase. Leave the last word out and see if the child will fill it in – for example, 'Ready, steady, go!' 'One, two, three!' Always say the last word with great enthusiasm and quite loudly so the child knows it is important.

- You can make car and animal or other relevant noises when playing or reading books. You can say 'Wheeee!' when the child goes down the slide, 'Brooom brooom!' when he pushes a car, 'Mooo!' when he plays with a cow puppet. *Old Macdonald had a farm* is an excellent song to encourage a child to make sounds.

- When doing an activity such as posting shapes, you could say 'Gone!' as each shape drops through the hole. When the child is used to this routine, leave a gap to see if he will fill in the word.

- When playing on the slide or climbing frame, use words to describe what the child is doing but stress one word – for example, '*Up* the ladder!', '*Down* the slide!' Alternatively, you could simply say 'up' and 'down', repeating the words with an up and down expression. You also have opportunities to practise these words when playing with cars, play people or a doll's house. Work on particular key words and make sure that all adults interacting with that child know which words to emphasise.

- Use opportunities to label things the child is using and stress the important words. Make sounds interesting – for example, 'Yoghurt! Yum, yum!'

- If a child is using a number of single words, try to extend them into familiar phrases by using adjectives – 'big bird', 'yellow pencil', 'dirty hands'. Introduce the words as often as possible in everyday contexts. Verbs can also be added to nouns to make longer phrases – 'drink milk', 'eat the biscuit', 'Jack's dancing!' for example.

- Encourage the child to use short phrases by using words such as 'more', as in 'more drink', or 'gone', as in 'drink gone'. Repeat the word or phrase whenever suitable opportunities arise. Use gestures to support what you say.

- Many children with autistic spectrum disorders are echolalic, which means they repeat whatever is said to them. They often do this without its having a meaning, but it is a good start because you know they can say the words and you can use the fact that they will copy you to encourage and extend their vocabulary. Use a lot of repetition, with the same phrases being built into daily routines until the child begins to understand what he is repeating and give it meaning.

Ideas for children who are using sentences

Some children may be able to speak quite well but are not able to have a conversation or give information that is not related to their own interests and needs. They do not have the idea of language as social interaction and cannot understand that you may be interested in something they did if they themselves are no longer interested in it.

They may also have difficulty recalling information and need a visual or verbal reminder of an event that has happened in the past (which may be five minutes ago) in order to talk about it.

The ideas given below can help develop the skills of these children.

- Try sending the child on a small errand with another child or adult and then ask him to tell you about it. At first you may have to prompt all the answers or use visual prompts, but, after some practice, he will be able to tell you what he did in two or three sentences.

- For example, you ask the child to go to the office with the classroom assistant to take the register. On his return, you pretend to have forgotten what you asked him to do and say, 'Where have you been?' The answer may need to be prompted – 'To the office' then 'Why did you go to the office?' to which he replies 'I took the register'. 'Who was in the office?' you say and 'Mrs Jones' is the reply

- After a time, you should be able to withdraw the prompts and the child may begin to volunteer more information spontaneously. Returning with a visual cue or object (a written message, a book) may prompt the conversation.
- Give a child a toy or object and ask him to tell you three things about it. He may tell you 'It's a cow' and you will have to prompt the rest by asking what colour it is and how many legs it has, or what sound it makes. However, in time, you will be able to gradually withdraw the prompts.
- It is useful to have visual prompts to help a child tell you about something he has done. You could ask his parents to send in some reminders of what he did at the weekend. For example, if he went shopping and then to have a hamburger, he could bring in a shopping bag and a burger wrapper. On school trips and special school activities, it is particularly important to have a photographic record and examples of what the child has done so he can tell others about it. A visual reminder of a trip to the seaside could include shells, a train ticket and some suncream. Anything that will trigger memory and help the child talk about his experience.

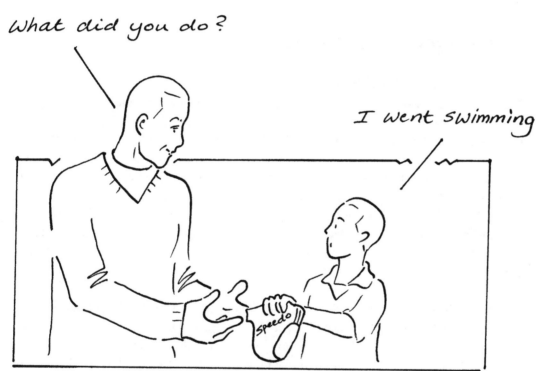

For a more able child, you could practise having conversations that you start, rather like a turn-taking game. You could have a microphone that goes back and forth to encourage the conversation and emphasise whose turn it is. You say the opening line, the child then makes a comment and you go back and forth until you run out of things to say. Better still, play it as a game with one or two other children, where they have to have a conversation and you give them the first line. You may need to prompt the answers at first:

'I like playing football.'
'I like playing on my computer.'
'I played football at the weekend. Our team won 4-1.'
'I played Star Wars on my computer with my friend and I won.' (And so on.)

Use picture cards and storybooks to encourage language development. When reading a story, ask a question about what might happen next. Look at pictures in magazines and books and talk about what you say. Use 'Why?', 'Where?' and 'Who?' questions. For example, 'Why is the car dirty?' 'Why is the girl wearing a helmet?' What has happened to the dog?' 'Who has eaten all the porridge?'

Some children find these questions very hard to answer and may need prompting. If children have difficulty answering questions about pictures, try using photographs taken in the playground and on outings or ask questions about real situations. For example, try writing with a broken pencil and say, 'Why won't my pencil write?'

If you have access to a digital camera, this is a very good way to present a visual reminder of an event that has just happened that has many benefits for language and learning. For example, a science experiment could be photographed and the pictures used to encourage written and spoken language, sequencing and to reinforce what has happened in the lesson.

Using signs and symbols

Why use signs and symbols?

Signs and symbols support spoken language and help develop communication, language and literacy skills. When you speak to a child with communication difficulties, whether or not he understands will depend on the context in which the statement was made, the tone of voice in which it was said and non-verbal communication cues, such as body language and gestures. If a teacher says 'Line up,' and all the children stand up and go to line up, the child will follow, as this is a routine that is repeated several times a day. If a mother goes to her child, points to his feet and says 'Get your shoes', he will run and get his shoes because she has pointed to his feet. He knows he has to put his shoes on before they go out and he is very motivated to do what her gesture intimates because he always enjoys going out.

Children with autistic spectrum disorders may pick up on contextual cues because they are tuned in to routines and know what happens within them. However, that does not mean they have understood the verbal instruction or even that they understand the reason for doing what they are asked. A child will line up with the others in his class, but his idea of where he is going might be based on previous knowledge of familiar routines. He may think it is dinnertime and then be very distressed when he finds himself in assembly. Some other communication system is essential to help this child understand what is going to happen and support the spoken word.

Signs or symbols?

Children with autistic spectrum disorders have difficulty reading body language and facial expressions and often have poor eye contact, so looking at a person when they are speaking can be difficult for them. For this reason, it is usually easier to use symbols to support language and teach communication skills than it is to use signs. However, the latter can be used to support routines – for example, to show the child he is going to be taken to the toilet or being asked to sit down or come to the teacher. Similarly, gestures can be used. Indeed, exaggerated gestures can be very helpful, even when the child is not looking, as he may see them in his peripheral vision and respond accordingly.

Children often learn one sign and use that for everything. Signs taught at snacktime may include 'biscuit', which is an inexpensive snack that most children enjoy, and 'please' or 'thank you', which are easy signs to prompt and do. It is important to note that it is not a good idea to teach children to sign or to say 'please' and 'thank you' when they have a very small vocabulary as they will use it to ask for everything they want and will then have difficulty learning names, signs or symbols to communicate their needs. Use opportunities to develop and extend communication skills, not to make it too easy.

Using symbols

Symbols are line drawings with written words at the bottom. You can use your own drawings, pieces of packaging or pictures cut out of books and magazines. However, once you have the computer software (and many schools do now), it is easy to make symbols of any size and to use them at home and school. They do not require specialist knowledge and, as they have the word written under the picture, they can be used to support literacy skills as well as language skills.

Children with autistic spectrum disorders often have good visual awareness. Temple Grandin, a woman with autism, has written about how she sees things in pictures. She describes how she sees concepts by picturing an example of that concept (a *hot* fire). This supports the view that symbols are a good choice if you are looking for a communication system for a child with autism.

Symbols can be used to support written information for children with poor literacy skills. For young children who are good readers, symbols clarify the meaning of written information and make it easier to understand. Many children who become fluent at reading with symbols can cope very well if the symbols are changed, particularly if it is something concrete like 'car' rather than something abstract like 'as' or 'the'.

Children who have fairly good language skills but poor literacy skills find symbols give them confidence in reading so that they begin to have more success in reading words. Texts can then be written with a combination of words with or without symbols. Symbols make abstract texts more accessible to children with literacy and comprehension difficulties and they can also type or dictate their own work using a symbols programme and read it back to their teacher, parents or peers.

Picture Exchange Communication System (PECS)

This is a system of teaching communication skills to children who have autistic spectrum disorders. It was developed in the US by psychologist Andrew Bondy and speech and language therapist Lori Frost and is now used by speech and language therapists throughout the UK. The system is very intensive to begin, as two adults are needed, and it is taught at home, school and used everywhere the child goes.

Frost and Bondy found that using PECS had the unexpected outcome of helping children speak as well as giving them a communication system that is easy to use. This helps the child feel less frustrated and more in control of his environment, giving the additional benefit of making him calmer and happier.

PECS can be used with any child who is not using language to communicate. This includes children who have some words but do not use them consistently or in a communicative manner. Thus you can use it with a child who will, for example, feel thirsty and say 'drink' while standing alone in the playground looking at his feet.

PECS teaches children to be active partners in a c o m m u n i c a t i v e exchange. They are taught to take a symbol to an adult to ask for something they want. When they are proficient at doing this, they are taught to use concepts ('I want the big biscuit'), adjectives ('I want the clean car') numbers and so on and to comment on things they hear ('I hear a telephone'), see ('I see a yellow duck') and feel ('I feel thirsty'). PECS can also be used to encourage communication between peers and support the development of turn-taking and play skills.

PECS should be taught by adults who have been trained to use it correctly. If it is not, children can become dependent on physical and verbal prompts that will prevent them developing spontaneous communication skills.

Communication board with Symbols

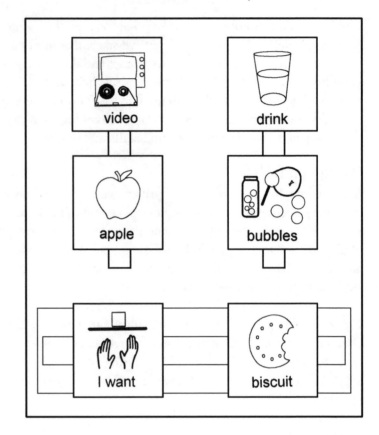

Examples of symbols used as visual reminders

All symbols from Widgit: Writing with Symbols 2000 (see resources)

listen

quiet

help

sit down

no thanks

no swimming

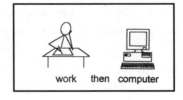

work   then   computer

Early learning: prerequisite skills

It is important when a child with an autistic spectrum disorder starts nursery or school to assess their strengths and needs in order to draw up a short individual education plan straight away. You may have a speech and language therapist, specialist teacher or educational psychologist to help you. If you have to wait for these services, it is important to know where to start.

Where you start will depend on the child's age and the setting you are in, but the first section in Chapter 1, Learning to play: building a relationship, is a good beginning for a young child. It is important not to wait too long for the child to 'settle' before setting short-term targets. If you find the child develops skills faster than you expected, it does not matter – it only takes a short time to set new targets. Remember, small steps are best, then important skills are not overlooked.

This section suggests strategies to develop early skills that are important for learning:

- Using rewards and praise
- Teaching a child to sit down
- Teaching a child to wait
- Motivating a child
- Developing attention and concentration
- Developing imitation skills
- Modelling and prompting
- Forward and backward chaining
- Generalising skills and knowledge.

Let us look at each of these in turn.

Using rewards and praise

Children with autism do not have an in-built desire to please others. They often do not understand why they should do something they do not want to do. They may feel anxious when asked to do something unfamiliar and prefer to do activities they know and enjoy, ones that feel safe and help them feel secure.

To encourage children to complete tasks you want them to do – particularly if it is unfamiliar or difficult for them – it is often necessary to give a reward. At first the reward must be something that is very motivating, so, for young children that may involve giving them a favourite toy or food item. Initially it should be something that can be given frequently and taken away (or eaten) in a very short time. Food can be broken into small pieces so that children are not being filled up with junk food between meals. Some children have particular interests or obsessions that can be used as a reward for doing what you want. For example, if Ben completes his writing satisfactorily he can look at the big book of flags until playtime.

Chapter 2

Rewards should always be given together with praise. When you praise a child, you must sound and look happy so the child understands your meaning even when they do not understand the words you have said. Praise should be clear and precise – for example, 'good looking', 'good sitting', 'very good try', 'great drawing!'

Rewards and praise should be given immediately the child gives the correct response or completes the activity satisfactorily. A child can be rewarded for working by being told they can 'go and play' or go to the computer or some other favourite activity. He should know that when he has completed the task he will get the reward and this may be put on his timetable at school or on a visual chart at home. Food rewards may be needed with young children but they should be phased out and replaced with non-food rewards when the child has become used to following instructions and is generally co-operative. Schools will not usually allow food to be used as a reward so try to substitute a favourite toy or activity before the child starts school.

As children grow older, more sophisticated systems of rewards can be put in place as they learn to wait for their reward. They could have tick charts or sticker books where they have to fill a certain number of boxes and are then given a special reward. The chart or book should say clearly what the reward (token, tick, sticker) is given for and this should be explained verbally or visually. This system works best when parents are also involved and encourage their child with interest and praise. It is important that reward charts and sticker books are designed to allow bad days to happen without upsetting the child's motivation and make them feel the reward will never come. Do not take stickers away for bad behaviour but be positive in your expectation that, although today was terrible, tomorrow will be better.

See also Chapter 8, Behaviour support strategies.

Teaching a child to sit down

When a child with an autistic spectrum disorder comes into nursery or school, one of the first things he will need to be taught is to sit down when asked to do so. The school environment will be particularly stimulating for him, as he may have heightened sensory awareness and find the sounds, smells and colours in the room are quite overwhelming. He may not understand why he should sit down when the other children do or feel that it is important to please the teacher and do as she asks. However, sitting down is a very important skill to learn and a prerequisite to many early learning activities at school and at home.

When a child is sitting, he is more able to focus on what is in front of him and not become distracted by other things happening around him. He also knows that when he sits, he is expected to do something – listen to a story, draw a picture, do a puzzle, cut some paper. A table and chair create a boundary around him that is important for a young child in helping him to pay attention to the task at hand.

What you can do

Begin by having a suitably sized table and chair in a quiet area of the room. Have some very motivating toys on the table and see if the child will sit by himself to explore the toys. If not, try a little prompt – pat the chair and say 'sit down'. Praise the child if he sits by saying 'Good sitting!' and immediately show him what wonderful things you have.

Some children will run up to the table, take the most exciting thing off it and run away to play with it. You will then have to take the toy, say 'my turn' in a firm voice and try to tempt the child back to the table to play with the toy. Sometimes you may have to show him what is expected by sitting him on the chair and immediately rewarding him with the toy and the phrase 'Good sitting!'

Very young or very active children may need food or drink rewards to teach them to sit. If so, go ahead and use them. They can be phased out and replaced by exciting toys.

Build up the time you expect the child to sit from a few seconds to eat a snack or flick a switch, and up to 20 minutes or more to complete a number of activities you want to work on with him. For a school-age child, you will want him to sit for the same time as his peers, although he may need some work adapted to meet his learning needs.

Sitting in groups

This can be difficult for young children with autistic spectrum disorders. They may be sensitive to the closeness of others around them and feel uncomfortable. In assembly, large spaces can make them feel panicky. They may not understand what is being said by the teacher or that the teacher is talking to them or that they are expected to listen quietly and pay attention. They may feel they have to sit there for ever, which will make them feel anxious.

Here are some ideas to try.

- Sit the child on the edge or front of the group near the teacher.
- A very young child may need to sit on an adult's knee at first. When the child is used to the routine of sitting on the carpet, he can then gradually be moved on to the floor or a chair.
- If the child is restless sitting on the carpet, sit him on a chair and have an adult sitting in a small chair behind him, lightly holding him.
- Some children find sitting in a large group is easier if they know where to sit. Have a mat or cushion marking where they should sit on the carpet.

- Remind the child verbally and visually (using a symbol or gesture) to sit quietly and listen.
- If the teacher is reading a story, try to give the child a copy of the book or a toy that symbolises the story, such as a teddy bear or doll to be Goldilocks.
- Use gestures, physical and verbal prompts to help the child join in with songs.
- When asking questions, remember that the child with an autistic spectrum disorder may not realise he is expected to answer unless he is spoken to by name. Therefore, use his name to gain attention before asking the question. Remember, too, that if you say his name at the end of the sentence, it is too late – the question will be lost.
- If a child is disturbing others in the group during carpet time, and if you have enough help, consider taking him out with one or two other children and covering the same topic with more direct teaching and sensory input. For example, make a story more real by illustrating it with things to hold, smell and feel, or slow down the pace of a maths lesson and use real examples or prepare for a science lesson one step at a time.
- In assembly, sit the child on the end of the row so he can leave easily if he is having difficulty sitting still. A small chair or cushion may be necessary to show the child he should remain sitting in one place.
- Have clear targets for the child and gradually build up the time he is expected to sit in a group. If he has poor language and listening skills and does not understand what is happening in assembly, what are you hoping to achieve by having him sit there? Is he ready to learn to sit quietly and listen in a large group? Is it helping develop his social interaction skills? If not, and there is somebody available to work with him in the classroom, it may be a good time to do some individual work in language or other basic learning skills instead.

See also Chapter 3, Structured teaching, and Chapter 8, Behaviour support strategies.

Teaching a child to wait

Children with autistic spectrum disorders sometimes have difficulty understanding that something is going to happen in the near future. They think that if it is not happening now, then it is not going to happen at all. This can make them feel anxious and, in some children, the anxiety and frustration can result in a tantrum or aggressive behaviour.

What you can do

The best way to deal with this is to teach the child to wait. 'You will need a wait symbol', which should be large and brightly coloured with the word 'wait' written on it. Cut out several that are identical and laminate them, as they will be needed in any situation where the child has to wait. Have at least one at school and several at home – perhaps one in each room of the house (especially the kitchen) and one in the car. Put some time aside every day to teach the concept of waiting.

To begin with, it is best to use a very motivating reward, such as bubbles, chocolate or a spinning top. Show the child what you have and ask if he wants it. For example, say 'Blow bubbles?' and blow lots of bubbles. When the child shows you he wants more bubbles say 'Wait' firmly and, at the same time, put the wait card in front of the child or give it to him to hold. Start by counting to five then say, 'Good waiting!' and blow some more bubbles.

Gradually increase the time the child has to wait before he is given what he wants. Do not increase the time too fast as the child may lose interest or become distressed. Go at a pace that feels right, and remember to use the verbal 'wait' as well as the visual prompt each time. Use the 'wait' sign with many different activities and in many different situations.

When you feel the child can wait for a reasonable length of time, which will vary depending on their age and understanding, you may find you can stop using the visual prompt (the 'wait' card) and just say 'Wait'.

Children who become anxious when they have to wait may benefit from a timer, so they know how long they have to wait, or a card that says 'wait for dinner' using symbols or words as necessary.

 for

Motivating a child

It can be difficult to motivate children with autistic spectrum disorders to attempt different activities, complete tasks or follow instructions. They do not have an intrinsic desire to please others and will not see the point of many activities they have to do, both at home and school.

Some will not understand why they have to come in from play, so the end of play will always result in some antisocial behaviour. Others, used to having certain things done for them, will need positive encouragement to learn to do it themselves.

Some children with autism feel discouraged from trying something new in case they make a mistake – a situation they can find hard to cope with. Even the knowledge that everyone else is applying themselves to a task will not always be enough to motivate them to give it a try.

What you can do

Have a system of rewards and give the child the clear message 'Work now, play later.' In other words, finish this task and then you can play with the train for ten minutes.

It is easier if rewards are shown visually. The child needs to know what they have to do and what will happen when they have finished. Have a visual timetable that shows that less enjoyable tasks are followed by things that are more enjoyable.

Make sure the work the child is doing is within their ability. Some children in mainstream schools are having to go too fast and complete a lot of work they do not understand because teachers are under pressure to cover the National Curriculum. Try to differentiate tasks whenever possible and give concrete examples. On the other hand, avoid giving work that is too easy – for example, always giving them the same worksheet as the others but only expecting them to do the colouring in.

Sit the child somewhere where there are fewest distractions. It can be helpful to sit a child with autism with a more able group of children as then he has good role models and peers who can help him. Although it is more practical to sit all the children needing extra help in one group, it sometimes becomes the noisiest and most distracting group and so does not help the child's learning or motivation.

Warn the child in plenty of time when an activity he enjoys is about to end and prepare him for the next, less interesting task. A traffic light system can be helpful here – that is, a green circle means the start of the activity, orange means it is nearly time to finish and red means stop and change activities. You could also use a timer to show how time passes.

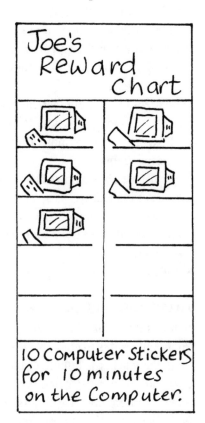

Check that the child has understood the instructions. Children with autistic spectrum disorders have difficulty following complex instructions or instructions that are given to a group.

With a young child, remember to make rewards immediate. Gradually increase the time he has to wait for the reward or the number of ticks he has to collect in order to get it, so that as he gets older he can wait for the reward to come at the end of the day or week.

Work closely with the child's parents. They will tell you if something has upset the child before coming in to school or if he slept badly. You can then subtly make fewer demands or build in more relaxation time to allow for this.

Developing attention and concentration

There are many reasons for children with autism having difficulty paying attention in the classroom. They may have heightened sensory awareness so that certain everyday sounds, colours, smells and textures will fascinate, distract or disturb them. People with autistic spectrum disorders who have written about their experiences often talk about their sensory difficulties and how uncomfortable and overwhelming they can be.

What you can do

Here are some things you could try to help increase a child's concentration span.

Sit the child in the least distracting area of the room, away from the door and the computer (see Chapter 3, Structured teaching).

Try not to shout! It can be very distressing for a child with an autistic spectrum disorder and it can confuse him. If your voice rises at the end of a sentence, that may be what he responds to, even if the beginning of the sentence was 'I told you not to ... '.

Be sensitive to the child's needs when introducing new experiences. He may need a gradual introduction to paint and dough, music or PE. Do not give up, but take it step by step, offering plenty of encouragement.

Try to organise a regular place for the child to go if things in the classroom get too difficult for him. A session in a corner of the classroom, listening to a tape through headphones, can be enough to block out difficult noises and calm the child down.

Another important reason for a child exhibiting poor attention and concentration is a lack of interest in what he is doing. Although some children with autistic spectrum disorders want to emulate their peers and follow school rules rigidly, others may not want to do anything that does not fit within their range of interests.

Here are a few small practical changes you can make.

- Make rewards very motivating and do not make the child wait so long for a reward that it never seems to come.
- Ensure the child knows how much work he has to do and what is going to happen when he has finished.
- If possible, adapt the work to include the child's interests – for example, if he loves trains and is learning to use a number line, make the number line into a train with carriages or even a railway line.
- Take things step by step and build the work up at a pace that suits the child.

Attention and classroom skills

Some children may not realise what is expected of them in the classroom. They will not know, unless it is made very clear to them, that they should listen to the teacher. They might think the teacher is talking to the other children, not to them. They might not realise when they should start work and how much work they should do. It is also important to realise that they might not have understood the verbal instructions given by the teacher or that they perhaps have difficulty remembering a sequence of instructions.

If this happens, try the following steps.

- Using the child's name and pausing before giving the instruction is the best way to make sure he hears what you say. For children with good language skills, you may be tempted to use longer or more complex sentences, but only do so if it is necessary.
- When the teacher is talking, you could give the child a visual reminder to listen to what is being said. It can either be a symbol (a drawing), a sign (hand cupped around your ear) or a written reminder.

- Use concrete examples where possible, particularly with young children.
- Keep verbal instructions brief, stressing the main words. If a child can only follow one

verbal instruction at a time, it is important to give the instructions one at a time.
- Make sure the child can see what he has to do and check that he has understood. If he can read, it is better to write the instructions down in a list. He can then cross off each step as it is completed.
- Use a lot of praise, especially with younger children, saying 'good sitting', 'good looking', 'good writing', 'good work' and so on.

If a child will not settle

We all have a bad day sometimes. If a child with autism is having a bad day and is very inattentive, it may be better to give him a break than to make the situation worse by waiting until he has disrupted other children and created an incident in the classroom. If he is in reception, could he do something relaxing in the nursery for a while? If he has adult support in class, could he go for a walk, on an errand or to the library? Maybe he could take his work and finish it in a quiet, empty room. Whatever you choose to do, do it calmly before there is a crisis.

It is important not to take the child away from his work and give him something that is normally given as a reward. Try to find other distractions, if that is what is needed. The reward must be earned, although it is perfectly fine to give it for effort rather than success. A very small task can require huge effort when we are having a really bad day.
See also Chapter 3, Structured teaching, and Social stories, page 83.

Developing imitation skills

Children learn some new skills by copying others. This is difficult for many children with autistic spectrum disorders. They may learn to copy things that fascinate them, like favourite scenes in Disney videos, or things that are odd and have caught their attention, like the way their baby sister eats her porridge, but they have difficulty copying important things like language, play and social interaction skills. You may stand in front of a child waving and saying, 'Wave bye bye', but the chances are he will look puzzled and fail to respond or make an attempt that is not quite right.

Most important is your awareness. If you remember that you have a child who has difficulty copying you, then you will not depend on it when teaching a new skill. Some children with autistic spectrum disorders will copy their peers rigidly as they like things to be fixed and orderly. However, they will often copy without understanding so they still need extra help to make their actions meaningful.

What you can do

With young children, play games where you copy their sounds and actions and see if they respond. The child may be taken aback and look as though he has just noticed your presence. When you are sure you have his attention, copy him and change it a little to see if the child will copy you. (See Learning to play: building a relationship, page 15).

Try making exaggerated sounds or do things that are funny, such as pulling faces in the mirror, pretending to be a ghost or blowing raspberries. Have two similar hats that are noticeable because they are very big, very bright, very furry. Put your hat on and look in the mirror. Then give the mirror to the child and see if he will copy you with the other hat.

In a more formal learning situation when you want a child to copy, always use short phrases and clear language. 'Do this' is a useful phrase in this context, followed by a clear example of what you want the child to do. The child learns that 'do this' means 'copy what I am doing.' You may say 'Clap!' or 'Wave!', demonstrating the action or including it in a game or song. You may need to use a physical prompt to teach the child what to do and gradually withdraw the prompt.

It is important to remember that teaching a child to copy is not the same as teaching the meaning of what he is copying. When children learn by imitation, it is the social context in which they learn it that teaches them a great deal more than the physical skill alone. They will be learning how others respond, what they expect and what meaning it has. If you say, 'Do this,' and wave, and the child copies you, he will still have to learn the social context of waving. This includes, for example, that it is a way of saying goodbye: you look at the other person when you do it and the other person usually says 'Goodbye' and waves back.

Even with a verbal child, it is better to keep language to a minimum as the child will find it easier if you give an example of what he is supposed to do, rather than a lengthy verbal explanation. If you are teaching him to sort fruit into apples, pears and oranges, you can demonstrate what to do by simply using the words, 'apple', 'pear' and 'orange' and show where the fruit has to go. You may extend this by saying 'apple with apple', 'pear with pear', but do not be tempted to give a longer explanation. 'Now ... you have to put all the apples together in the red dish and all the pears go together in the green dish and the oranges have to go here in the orange dish. Do you think you could do that for me?' would overwhelm a child.

Children who have difficulty drawing are often able to do so if you draw the picture bit by bit (head, body, arms, legs, face) and they copy it step by step. For some children, this develops into some creative drawing of their own. It can be helpful if you divide the paper in half with a thick line and do your drawing on your half so they can see clearly that there are two sides – one for you and one for them.

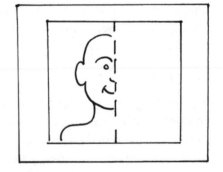

This strategy can also be useful when teaching construction or matching skills. Then, you sit facing the child and give a step-by-step example on your side and the child sits and copies each step on his side until he has learned what to do independently. There is no creativity in teaching skills this way, but you can work up to that by turning your copying activity into a turn-taking game, where you each place a piece on the item you are building and see how it turns out.

Repetition is important, especially with a young child. You may think that he is never going to drink that pretend cup of tea or wave goodbye or draw a picture. One day, though, it will happen – often when you are not watching.

Prompting and modelling

Prompting, modelling, and shaping are techniques that can be used to teach skills in a structured, step-by-step process. They are particularly important for children with autistic spectrum disorders who often have poor imitation skills and do not understand what they have to do.

They have difficulty following spoken instructions and cannot imagine the practical or pleasurable outcome of learning a new skill. For example, if you want to teach a young child to pedal a trike, you may find it more difficult than you expect and give up quite quickly. The child is physically capable of pedalling but does not understand what is expected or why. He sits on the trike and plays with the bell or rocks back and forth on it a few times and then gets off. You know that, if he could learn, he would have such fun, independently pedalling around the playground or park.

Prompting

In order to teach a child how to pedal a trike, you will need to use a physical prompt. In other words, you put his feet on the pedals, put your hands over them and push them around. Do this slowly, as much as the child will tolerate each day, until he gains confidence. As you push his foot down on the pedal, also use a verbal prompt – 'Push! Push!' Then, gradually withdraw the physical prompt by making it lighter, so the child has to use more effort to pedal, but not so light that he gives up. It should then be possible to withdraw the physical prompt and just use the verbal prompt until the child can pedal with no help at all.

This technique can be used for teaching most physical skills, particularly if the child is having difficulty imitating or understanding verbal instructions. The hardest but most important thing to do is withdraw the physical prompt as soon as possible as, otherwise, children can become dependent on it. A verbal prompt is a good initial back-up, but it too can gradually be withdrawn or replaced by a sign or gesture.

Modelling

This technique is used for children who are able to copy what you do. You show the child what to do, then ask them to copy you. If he is unable to copy or makes an error, you may want to show him again or use a physical or verbal prompt to help him complete the activity successfully.

Shaping occurs when you change a child's skills or behaviour in small steps to reach a desired target. For example, if he always makes circular marks on paper, you can show him how to draw a circle then a face, then other circular drawings like an apple, a cat or a snowman. If he likes making the sound mamama you could start by copying the sound and change it to mum then mummy, or if he waves his hands to music you might show him how to clap. Shaping is a natural response when teaching young children and should be used consistently with plenty of praise for each new step.

Hand over hand

If you are working with a child who does not mind being touched, some skills can be taught by putting your hands over the child's and doing it with him. This can be helpful when teaching skills that require manipulation and fine motor skills, such as taking lids off pots, using switches, using a knife and fork, using a pencil or paintbrush.

Again, it is most helpful to gradually take your hands away so the child can do the last step unaided, then the last two steps and so on.

Forward and backward chaining

Forward and backward chaining is a technique for teaching new skills, particularly to children who have difficulty with organisation skills, attention or language. The aim is to break the task you are teaching down in to smaller components and make sure the child achieves success before becoming frustrated.

Forward chaining

This technique is used when you break things down into small steps and teach the child the first step in the chain. When he has mastered the first step, you teach the next step and so on. For example, if you want to teach a child to tie his shoelaces, you will teach the first step of crossing over the laces and then finish tying them yourself. When the child had mastered crossing the laces, you teach him to make the first loop, then the second and so on. At each stage, praise his progress and he will feel he has achieved something positive.

Backward chaining

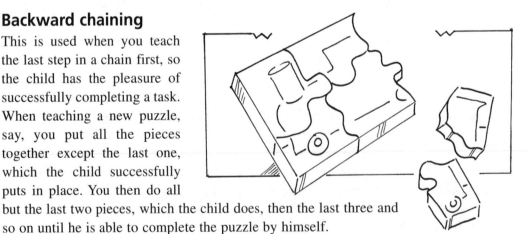

This is used when you teach the last step in a chain first, so the child has the pleasure of successfully completing a task. When teaching a new puzzle, say, you put all the pieces together except the last one, which the child successfully puts in place. You then do all but the last two pieces, which the child does, then the last three and so on until he is able to complete the puzzle by himself.

Backward chaining builds confidence and is rewarding for the child. It is possible to teach many skills this way. For example, threading beads is a complex skill that requires both hands to work together. It is easier to teach the child to pull the lace through a bead before teaching him how to thread the lace into the bead. You can divide the task into steps:

- you hold the bead and push the lace in, the child pulls it through
- you hold the bead, the child pushes the lace in and pulls it out the other end
- the child holds the bead, pushes the lace in and pulls the lace out.

Each stage might take some time for the child to learn. Do not keep going over the same thing day after day if the child is not progressing at all and you feel you are not moving on. Look for other activities that are easier and may be a 'stepping stone'. In the example given of threading beads, try lacing toys, cotton reels, threading on to dowel, threading pasta and different sizes and shapes of beads.

Sometimes it is easier to teach a skill in a different order to the one that follows naturally. If it is easier to do it this way and it will still give the child a sense of accomplishment, then go ahead and do it. The important things to remember are:

- break the task into small steps
- teach the child one step at a time
- be consistent – do not have a different adult teaching the child to use a knife and fork in a different way every day
- make sure success is built in to the process
- use a lot of praise.

Generalising skills and knowledge

Children with autistic spectrum disorders are very rigid in their thinking. This means they have enormous difficulty transferring what they have learnt in one situation to other similar situations. Parents will say, 'She always eats with a knife and fork at home' and this will be news to the teacher, who will reply, 'That is strange – she doesn't seem to know what to do with a fork here. We have difficulty stopping her eating everything with her fingers.' Equally, further discussion may reveal several skills the child has learnt at school – undressing and dressing for swimming, for example – that the parents did not know their child could manage independently. This lack of ability to generalise one skill or piece of knowledge to other situations can be a serious difficulty when the teacher is not aware of just how rigid the child can be.

What you can do

This depends to some extent on the level of the child's understanding but, essentially, it is important to always generalise what you are teaching across a wide number of relevant situations and examples. For instance, you may be teaching language skills. You have a lovely picture of a house and teach the child 'This is a house.' You have to make sure that the child knows what real houses look like and that they come in all shapes and sizes. Picture books often show country cottages with sloping roofs, a smoking chimney and flowering climbers growing up the wall. However, many children live in terraced houses or blocks of flats that do not look at all like this.

Teaching in mainstream schools depends a great deal on the premise that children will quickly generalise what they have learnt across a wide number and variety of different situations. Make sure the child with an autistic spectrum disorder has opportunities to learn the same thing in different situations, beginning with a range of practical and relevant examples. If you have a child who can only subtract using small wooden blocks, he will need to practise that same skill using practical examples in different settings before moving on to learning more complex ideas.

Make sure that there is good communication between teachers, carers and parents so that children can practise new skills at home, nursery or school. A notebook that goes back and forth from home to school can be very helpful in keeping everyone up to date.

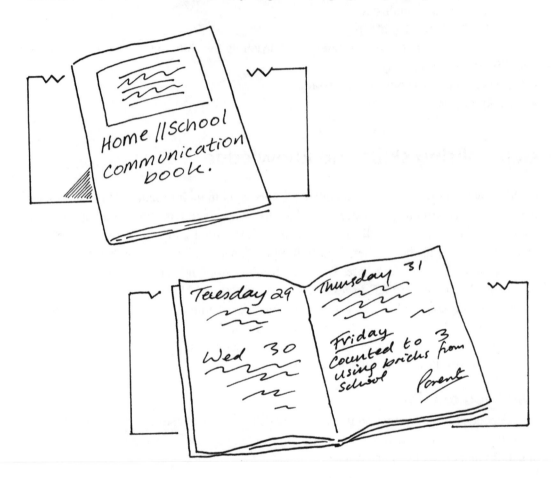

Chapter 3

Structured teaching

The idea of structured teaching is one aspect of teaching used in Treatment and Education of Autistic and related Communication-handicapped Children or TEACCH for short, which is based in North Carolina, USA. It is used in many forms in specialist schools and units for children with autistic spectrum disorders throughout the UK, adapted by teachers, parents or carers to suit the requirements of the child and the situation in which it is used.

The most important aspect of structured teaching is that the child can see exactly what the task is and what will happen when it is finished. He has a schedule showing the order of activities and tasks are presented visually so that he is clear what has to be done. For a very able child, this may mean that he has a written list of instructions detailing the task or activity. For a young child doing a sorting task, it may mean that there are several objects to sort and a visual prompt such as coloured bowls or big and little bowls to show how they should be sorted. Tasks and activities are based on the child's skills and needs and taught in a step-by-step way so that important prerequisite skills are not missed out.

Using structured teaching reduces anxiety and improves attention and motivation. It also discourages a high level of dependence on an adult. Organising work visually so that a child with autism can see what he has to do and not be distracted by unimportant details is always important and should be kept in mind whenever work is presented.

Structured teaching is particularly useful when you:

- have a distractible, inattentive or unhappy child
- want to teach a child to complete a task or series of tasks independently
- want to teach a new skill and the child is having difficulty understanding what he has to do.

Structured teaching is useful at home, too – particularly for teaching independent dressing and washing skills. In nursery, it helps calm an excitable child and provides a focus to learn new skills and work on specific developmental targets. As the child gets older, it helps develop independent working skills so he knows what is expected and does not constantly need an adult by his side.

The next few pages about structured teaching contain information under the following headings:

- Developing and using timetables and schedules
- How structured teaching is organised
- Meeting the needs of a child with autistic spectrum disorder in nursery or playgroup.

Developing and using timetables and schedules

Many children with autistic spectrum disorders need to know what is happening now and what is going to happen next. They find change difficult to deal with and can be distressed by unexpected events and cancellations. They often have difficulty organising themselves and can feel extremely anxious when faced with the unknown.

Timetables and schedules are therefore useful at home and school. A child at school who is familiar with the routine of the day will feel more relaxed when he can see it laid out in pictures or words in front of him. A child at home will have a structure to his day and will not feel he is 'free-wheeling' through time in a haphazard manner.

Timetables and schedules can use photographs, symbols, drawings or words, depending on what the child will understand. The important thing is that they are clear, unambiguous and do not give too much information at once. They can be written in list form on a sheet of paper or lined up on a strip of card. A schedule can be used to break down the school day or a single activity into manageable steps. It can be used at home to show the routine of the day, help organise and structure busy times or teach particular skills.

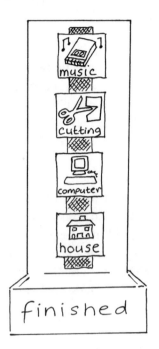

Making a timetable for a child in a nursery

Velcro is a wonderful invention that comes in very handy when you want to make a timetable for a young child. Make sure to laminate the symbols, photos and drawings you want to use so that they are tough and can be used time and time again.

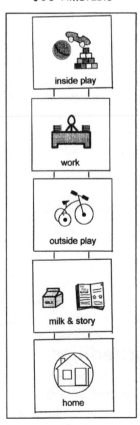

Jo's Timetable

For a young child starting nursery, a timetable using clear symbols or line drawings is best. The first thing to do is teach the child what the symbols mean. This can take several weeks, so start with a very simple timetable and use it consistently every day.

The different areas the symbols relate to should also be labelled with larger versions of the same symbols. So, the outside play symbol can be placed on the door to the outside, the milk and story symbol in an uncluttered space near the carpet, the home symbol near the exit and so on.

Have the pictures for the main activities of the day lined up from top to bottom or from left to right on a piece of card. The top 5 cm (2 in) of the card should be a different colour to the rest and it is helpful if you can make a small box or pocket at the bottom to keep the finished cards together. If not, a posting box or plastic wallet next to the timetable will do just as well.

You may have the symbols shown in the picture running from top to bottom on the timetable.

For terms such as 'inside play' and 'outside play', use a drawing of a favourite toy or activity used at these times.

At the beginning of the session, show the child her timetable, which should be on the wall somewhere accessible and away from visual distractions. At first, just talk about the top symbol. When the child understands the timetable, you can then point to each symbol and say what it is.

For children who enjoy looking at photographs, you may want to have a photo of the child doing each activity instead of (or in addition to) the symbols. However, make sure the photographs are clear and unambiguous, as a child may just look at one thing in the picture (for example, bubbles) that is not available every day.

Take the first activity symbol to the activity area and match it with the big symbol there. When the activity is finished, you go back to the timetable with the child and, saying 'Play finished', place that symbol in the box or pocket at the bottom or the plastic envelope fixed to the wall beside it. You then pick up the next symbol and show it to the child, saying 'work' and take it to match with the symbol in his structured work area.

If two activities run into each other and occur in the same place, such as milk and story, it is OK to put them on the same symbol or just to use one symbol that applies to both activities – maybe a circle of chairs.

If an activity is changed – outside play is not possible because it is raining very hard, for example – make sure that the symbol is changed on the timetable as soon as possible. Also, put a large red cross over the large outside play symbol that is on the door to the outside play area to show the child that there is no outside play today. This does not always calm the child, particularly a young child, and so other strategies may have to be organised in advance.

A cancelled swimming session can be particularly distressing and you may need to think in advance how to prepare the child for this and what activity can be used to replace it. Social stories (see page 83) can be helpful in preparing the child to understand what will happen if swimming is cancelled.

Note that, as a child learns what each symbol means, there is no need to match it to the various areas. Just have a different colour of card at the top of the timetable and place the symbol there.

Many children with autistic spectrum disorders who are in mainstream primary schools seem to manage very well without a timetable. They follow what the other children are doing and do not want to do anything that will make them feel different. However, if there is a change to their usual day or if they have a supply teacher, they may feel very anxious and find it difficult to concentrate. They become difficult and disrupt the class. Teachers can avoid this by having a class timetable that is clearly written up on the board twice a day at registration. If there is a last-minute change, it is then very easy to alter and the child then knows what is going to happen. This may also help other children in the class.

At home, schedules can be an enormous help in encouraging a child with an autistic spectrum disorder to organise himself. For example, they can help a child to get dressed and be ready for school in the morning or with the bedtime routine in the evening. In the same way, many children like to read television programme guides even though they know very well when their favourite programmes will be on. Having the guide gives them extra reassurance that nothing has changed.

This technique can be used to help with other weekly activities and outings, such as shopping, youth club, drama class and so on. It can be reassuring for the child to have a weekly schedule of these posted up somewhere. Use words, drawings or photographs, whatever is easiest for the child to follow, and be sure to keep it up to date. Think how you would feel if you lost your diary or forgot to put in important changes.

You can use schedules and lists to teach independence skills. For example, below is a list of instructions for a boy who can read well but gets very muddled when he has to use the toilet. He pulls off far too much paper and leaves it lying around the toilet. He gets in a mess and forgets to flush the toilet or wash his hands. Try writing a list like this and you realise just how complicated some things we do every day really are!

After doing a poo:

- stand up
- pull the toilet paper down to the red line
- tear the paper off at the green line
- bend over and wipe your bottom
- put the paper in the toilet
- take more paper down to the red line
- pull the paper off at the green line
- wipe your bottom again
- put the paper in the toilet
- pull up your pants
- pull up your trousers
- flush the toilet
- go to the basin and wash your hands with soap
- dry your hands
- go back to class or to play.

Lists and schedules giving instructions should be tried out several times with an adult to make sure the child knows what to do and check that the instructions are clear and unambiguous. It is surprising how difficult it can be to give clear, step-by-step instructions to a child who is unlikely to fill in any obvious omissions.

Other visual aids can also be used. In this case, the toilet roll holder is marked with a green line on the serrated edge. A red line is marked about 46 cm (18 in) down. The child is taught how to pull the paper to the red line and tear it at the green line, wipe his bottom and follow the instructions, which are stuck on the wall at eye level. Instructions like these can help other children, too.

How structured teaching is organised

Example 1

You have three-year-old Josephus in your nursery who flits around the room touching some things but rarely attempting anything new.

He likes to do puzzles and is so obsessed by numbers and letters he will spend a large part of his time gazing at posters of the alphabet and counting friezes.

You do have a special needs room, but he spends all his time in there looking at the number line on the wall. You want to move him on, but how can you do it?

What you can do

Make up a timetable with pictures, photographs or symbols showing the main events of the day. Include a 'work' symbol or photo.

Find a work area inside the classroom that has few distractions. Use screens, the back of shelving units and the wall to make the area as bare as possible. When Josephus is used to sitting there, he can begin to personalise it with his work.

- You will need two trays or boxes (in different colours) and five plastic wallets. Put two small pieces of Velcro on each plastic wallet and put a strip of Velcro on a piece of strong card.

- Have two sets of numbers, '1' to '5', laminated, with Velcro on the back. In addition, have a symbol or picture of something that Josephus really enjoys – in this case, an alphabet book.

- Stick one set of numbers in a line on the strong card and one number on each of the plastic wallets. Put the reward symbol after the '5'.

- Put one activity in each plastic wallet. Put exactly what Josephus will need in order to do that activity and no more. For example, if you only want him to have a choice of three coloured pens, just put three in. If you want him to thread five cotton reels, just put five in.

- Nothing should be confusing or ambiguous. Children with autistic spectrum disorders find it hard to know what is important and what is not. They can feel overwhelmed by a large number of colours, sizes and shapes and will not know where to start.

- Put all the plastic wallets, in order, in one box or tray. This is the 'work' box. Green is a good colour for this box.

- Put an activity Josephus is able to do at the beginning. This helps him to settle down and achieve success early on.

- Set up the work area with the work box on the left and the 'finished' box on the right. The strip of strong card with the numbers '1' to '5' on it should be in the middle where Josephus can reach it. The numbers can go from left to right or from top to bottom. Some children will not be able to match numbers so they should have five coloured simple shapes to match instead.

- Take Josephus to his timetable and show him the 'work' symbol before taking him to sit at his table. If possible, you should sit opposite him as he can see your face and follow your example. If that is not possible, sit beside him. Show him how to take the first card from the strip, match it to the first wallet in the work box and do the activity. Then, when it is completed prompt him to put it in the finished box. He then takes the second card and so on until he has completed all the activities.

- At first, you will have to show Josephus what to do by modelling and prompting. Keep your language clear and brief, using a lot of praise and stressing the main words – '*match* the card', '*open* the bag', '*good* writing', '*finished*.'

When you first introduce structured teaching, you may have to reward Josephus after every completed task. The reward should be something that does not take long and will not be distracting. Small pieces of food such as raisins are good or some bubbles. The big reward comes at the end, when all the tasks have been completed.

With a young child, it is most useful to use this structured time to teach new skills. When he has learnt a new skill, encourage him to practise it in the nursery alongside other children or in a small group. Generalise the skill using different materials or introduce it in a different context. For example, if he has learned to thread beads in the structured work sessions, teach him to thread cotton reels, pasta, plastic shapes and so on alongside his peers to make necklaces, belts, wiggly worms, Christmas decorations and so on.

Some children learn new skills very quickly using this method of teaching. If so, keep changing the activities in the structured sessions while ensuring they are being practised in the classroom. Even a short structured session of 20 to 30 minutes every day can be enough to calm a child, teach new skills and improve attention and concentration throughout the day.

Example 2

Joe is in year 3 and has adult support throughout the day. He has autism and dyspraxia and is dependent on his support worker.

Although his language and social skills are developing well, he is not able to read or write without the help of symbols.

Joe's memory is poor, he is dreamy and easily distracted by others. He likes to spin things and manages to find all kinds of things to spin when he should be working.

When Joe's support worker is away, he is left on his own to daydream and spin or is taken to the nursery to 'help', although this usually means he chooses an activity he enjoys and plays repetitively by himself.

What you can do

It is important that Joe learns to work independently. Every day, he should do some independent structured work that makes him practise skills he needs but which he does not find too difficult.

- Give Joe a work area in a quiet corner of the classroom. Have his work prepared for him so that he knows what to do and use symbols to support brief written instructions. Make sure he has what he needs near at hand or give him a pictorial list of what he has to collect.

- Gradually build up the time that Joe spends doing independent work. Start with ten minutes, then, as he achieves this, add five more minutes and so on until you have reached a time that seems reasonable for him.

- Give him enough work to fill the allotted time. Use a number strip as described above or use maths, writing, reading and other symbols. Put each workbook or activity in a plastic wallet in a work box and have a finished box too, as described above.

- Joe needs a very motivating reward. A good reward could be an extra special spinning toy that he is allowed to spin for ten minutes when he has completed all his work. He could also have a reward book from which he chooses his reward.

- It might be helpful to organise his work time so he gets extra minutes reward time if he finishes his work quickly and less reward time if he is very slow. He has the ability to understand this.

- Joe should also be encouraged to work with a group using peer support. He is able to read using symbols and can complete worksheets that require cutting, sticking, colouring, matching and joining pictures and dots. He can fill in the initial letter of words. As he becomes more used to working independently in his own work space, he will be able to transfer these skills to a group situation.

Example 3

Lily is seven years old and has autism. She attends her local primary school and is able to read simple texts.

She likes to do what the other children are doing, has good imitation skills and is not distracted by noise or activity. With some help from the teacher and her peers, she is able to cope independently in the class for a large part of the day.

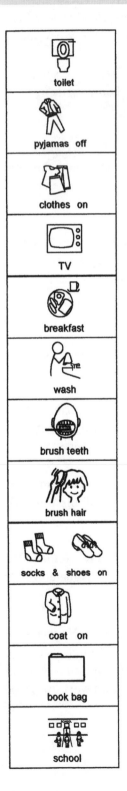

At home, however, she is not so independent. She has two younger siblings, aged five and three, and there is always a rush in the morning because Lily will not wash or dress herself for school so her mother has to do it for her. Physically, there is no reason for Lily not dressing herself as she manages to change for swimming without help and at school she will change for PE. There is plenty of time to dress herself in the morning as she wakes early and goes downstairs to turn on the television. This has been encouraged by the rest of the family so that they can have a little longer to sleep.

What you can do

Lily's parents will have to get up at the same time as Lily to teach her to follow a routine. However, when she has learned what to do, she will be able to manage independently.

- Lily should have a timetable showing the order of things she needs to do in the morning. This can be made using pictures and words or just words.

- The activities (shown here with a symbol and the word) are stuck with Velcro to a strip of card and she takes each one off and posts it in a finished box when she has done it.

- Lily is given two baskets in her bedroom. One is labelled 'pyjamas' and one is labelled 'clothes'.

- In the evening, Lily's clothes are placed in the basket in the order she needs to put them on. Using backward chaining (see page 50), she is taught that, in the morning, she is to take off her pyjamas, put them in the pyjamas basket and put her clothes on from the other basket. She still needs help with her shoes and socks so these are done later.

- In the bottom of the clothes basket is a big television picture. Lily learns that when she has reached this she is allowed to watch television.

- If Lily is watching television in her pyjamas when her parents get up, it is turned off and she is taken to her timetable, shown what she has to do and told to do it. If she makes a fuss, it is ignored. She is always praised when she has got herself dressed.

- When it is time to have a wash, Lily has two more baskets in the bathroom. One is labelled 'wash' and one 'finished'. In the wash basket is a flannel, hand towel, toothbrush, toothpaste and, at the bottom, a picture of a hairbrush. Using backward chaining, Lily is taught to wash herself in the morning with a minimum of help. When she has washed, her mother gives her some handcream as a reward – Lily loves to rub it on her hands.

At weekends and holidays, Lily has the same routine (dress first, then watch television), as she is not yet able to distinguish exceptions to the rule. However, once she has become comfortable with her dressing routine, she can be given a visual timetable each day, showing which days she has to get dressed before she watches television and the days when she can get dressed after breakfast. This will help her understand that days are different and not to become too insistent on having the same routine each day.

Lily enjoys going to school so that is a reward in itself. At weekends and holidays, she has a reward book that she chooses from when she has completed all the tasks on her schedule.

What these examples say

These three examples show some of the ways in which structured teaching can be used to help teach children with autistic spectrum disorder. It can help teachers and parents manage difficult behaviour in the classroom and at home because the children are calmer, they know what is expected and what is going to happen next. Although the technique depends on a motivating reward system, as the child becomes older and more confident, it is possible to introduce ticks or stickers, which they have to 'save up' for a reward.

Structured teaching can be adapted to most situations. Teachers in mainstream schools sometimes worry that it isolates the child from his peers. However, everything has to be a balance between meeting the child's complex needs and helping him learn alongside others. A child who constantly depends on adult help in order to feel secure or is unable to settle in a noisy classroom and focus on learning new skills needs structured teaching, but it should not take up the whole day.

Meeting the needs of a child with an autistic spectrum disorder in nursery or playgroup

Example 4

A three-and-a-half year old boy with autism has started at the nursery where you work as a teacher. You have wide experience of working with children with special educational needs but have never worked with a child with autism before.

You have been with the nursery nurse to meet the child, Yusef, at home. He has severe social and communication difficulties with no language and will make his needs known by pulling an adult towards what he wants or bringing a cup for a drink. He manipulates toys but does not play in a meaningful way, although he enjoys pushing switches repeatedly on musical cause and effect toys.

Yusef will do a familiar 12-piece inset puzzle unaided, although he cannot sit still for more than two or three minutes and will constantly leave an activity or meal to run up and down the room several times. His favourite activities at home are watching the music channel on television and running about at the park.

His parents say that, although his gross motor skills are good, he tends to push other children out of the way if they are climbing the slide when he is or they are in his path when he is running about. He does not realise the implications of hurting another child and will ignore the commotion he causes and carry on with what he is doing.

Yusef will be at nursery for 2½ hours each day. He will have 30 minutes daily support from a learning support assistant who has no training in autism, although she has worked with a child with a hearing loss. His parents have requested a statutory assessment of his special educational needs but they have not heard whether or not it has been agreed to. He is on a waiting list for speech and language therapy. How can you help him?

What you can do

If possible, organise some training for staff in the nursery in autistic spectrum disorders. Find out if your local authority has a specialist teacher for children with autistic spectrum disorders or a specialist nursery or primary school or unit you can visit for ideas. Contact The National Autistic Society, which will be able to send information about courses, useful publications and sources of support in your area.

Find out what is happening with the statutory assessment. Yusef is going to need extra adult support if he is to access the benefits of a mainstream nursery. You will need to assess whether or not his pushing behaviour will put other children at risk of being injured and if you need to ask for additional interim support while waiting for the statementing process to be completed.

Many schools now have symbols programs on their computers. If you have access to one, print off symbols for some of the main classroom areas and activities. Label each main area of the classroom with a large symbol (about 7 cm/3 in square). If you cannot find a symbols program, it would be a useful investment for the nursery, although clear, close-up photographs or line drawings can be used instead.

Think about where you could situate a quiet work area for Yusef. Preferably, this would be in the classroom, although, if he is very easily distracted, he may need to have a workspace outside the classroom to begin with.

Make up a timetable showing inside play, outside play and work. Place the drawings on a strip of card with Velcro. At first, show Yusef how to match the symbols with the large versions of the symbols in the respective areas. The large 'inside play' symbol can be placed somewhere uncluttered near his favourite activities. The 'outside play' symbol can be on the door to the outside play area. Increase the number of symbols you put on the timetable slowly. Too much information at once will be confusing and it may take several weeks for Yusef to understand what the symbols mean.

Find some noisy cause and effect toys that will interest Yusef immediately and some toys to use as rewards, such as bubbles, puzzles, musical toys.

Decide on consistent strategies to use to teach Yusef not to push other children. These would include teaching him to 'Wait' and to take turns with his peers, develop an awareness of others and slow down in the playground.

Write up an individual education plan for Yusef. Give him three or four short-term targets based on the information you have and the extra resources you can use. It may contain the following targets.

Baseline Yusef will sit briefly to begin activities he enjoys but does not remain seated.

Target Yusef will sit down when asked to do so and complete a short activity.

Strategy
- Put out a short activity that Yusef enjoys which has a clear completion point, such as a puzzle or a posting toy.
- Tell him to sit down. Praise him for 'good sitting.'
- Prompt him to stay sitting until he has finished his puzzle or do half the puzzle for him so he can finish it quickly. If he gets up, bring him back to his seat.
- When he has finished, praise him and stress that he has finished, saying, for example, '*Finished*, clever boy!'
- Repeat this several times throughout the morning using different activities.
- Gradually increase the length of time the activity will take.

Baseline Yusef rarely looks up when his name is called.

Target Yusef will look up when his name is called.

Strategy
- Call Yusef by name, maybe using a noisy toy to gain his attention. Reward him immediately he looks at you.
- Use motivating rewards, such as bubbles, spinning tops, noisy puppets.

Baseline Yusef plays on his own and ignores others around him.

Target Yusef will play interactive games with an adult.

Strategy
- Sit alongside Yusef and join in with what he is doing.
- Turn it into a turn-taking, interactive game.
- Sing about or copy what he is doing.
- When Yusef enjoys the game, encourage another child to join in.

Baseline Yusef manipulates toys but does not use them for pretend play. For example, he will play with the wheels of a car but will not push the car along the ground.

Target Yusef will begin to use favourite toys for pretend play.

Strategy
- Have an adult show Yusef how he can play with a toy he enjoys. Use noisy, exciting toys, including cars with sirens, cars that go fast when you push down a button, telephones with bells, toys in the home corner.

It is unlikely that Yusef will be able to sit on the carpet with the rest of the group, although he may do so with adult help. If he finds nursery very hard and his behaviour is difficult to manage, then set up a structured work session for him straight away and build up the time he is working with an adult in his own work space. However, if he copes well with playing and learning new skills alongside his peers, then structured work will not be necessary at this stage.

It is important that all the adults in the nursery work with Yusef from the beginning and are not put off by his 'leave me alone' attitude. It is easy to unintentionally create a situation where he builds a relationship with just one adult. Other adults need to play with Yusef as well and use any brief opportunity that arises to develop his interactive skills.

Suggested structured or tabletop activities for Yusef

Start by assessing what Yusef can do, then move him on to the next stage. When showing Yusef new skills:

- use consistent short instructions
- use modelling, prompting, forward and backward chaining
- when Yusef has mastered a skill, generalise what he has learnt to other activities in the nursery.

Here are some ideas.

- **Sorting objects** Have a number of small objects to be sorted into pots – for example, clothes pegs, crayons, beads, bottle tops, feathers. Start with two or three different objects: five clothes pegs, five beads, five feathers and three pots to sort them into. Show him what to do using modelling and physical prompting. When Yusef can sort three different objects, increase the number.

- **Sort objects by colour** Have a red, blue, green and yellow bowl and a number of small, coloured objects to sort into the bowls. Alternatively, use a pegboard with large pegs and model how you want the pegs sorted. Mosaic patterns are also good – where the pegs are placed according to a pattern underneath – but these require more skill.
- **Match real objects to photos, line drawings, symbols or silhouettes** Start with two drawings and two objects, then build up to ten.
- **Match pictures to pictures** It is easiest to do this using a lotto board with four clear pictures and matching cards or a board with strips of Velcro showing clearly where the pictures should be matched.
- **Match objects to shapes** Use different sizes of bottle tops and a board with the shapes drawn on one side in order of size, on the other with the shapes drawn randomly.
- **Introduce new inset puzzles, form boards, posting boxes and simple four- to six-piece jigsaw puzzles.**
- **Build a construction following simple visual instructions** Draw each step on a separate card and tie the cards together. Match the pieces to the ones on the card and add the next piece. Start with three simple pieces.
- **Thread** fat beads or cotton reels on to a lace or piece of dowel. Start with five beads.
- **Screw and unscrew lids** for example, put interesting items in screw-top pots – a little coloured glitter, balloons, sequins.
- **Introduce a number of different drawing implements.**
- **Cut and stick** starting with fringing or cutting thin strips of coloured or shiny paper.
- **Introduce new books** start with noisy or tactile books and lift the flap books.

It may take some time for Yusef to settle at nursery or at school and for staff to feel they have a relationship with him. If he finds the nursery environment overwhelming, and there are no adults available to support him during his time there, you may want to consider asking a family member to stay with him for some of the time, gradually decreasing in small steps as Yusef becomes more confident. If that is not possible, it may be necessary to introduce Yusef slowly to nursery, and build up the time he spends there from 5-10 minutes a day to a whole session.

A structured small step approach reduces anxiety in a child with autism and offers a means to succeed. It is predictable, it includes tangible rewards, and it encourages the use of techniques and strategies that are positive and successful for the child. In the long term, it provides an anchor during the day that helps a child with autism tackle new challenges and deal with more difficult aspects of his day.

Developing literacy skills

Children with autistic spectrum disorders often lack imagination. They have difficulty seeing life from somebody else's perspective. When they do seem to have a good imagination, this can be restricted to limited topics of special interest.

Young children with autism may have no interest in books except as objects. They sometimes have obsessions with certain books or catalogues and refuse to look at any other books or find it difficult to share a book and complain if you try to turn the book the right way up. They may also have difficulty learning to read and write. These skills are complex and require us to concentrate on several things at once.

This chapter is divided into the following parts:

- Developing an interest in books
- Teaching a child with autistic spectrum disorders to read
- Helping children with handwriting difficulties.

Developing an interest in books

If a child is only interested in certain books, such as catalogues or books with numbers and letters, these make a good starting point. However, you need to ensure that he moves on from this stage and does not become stuck.

You could use photographs of familiar people or pictures cut from catalogues to make books that will interest the child. Introduce others linked to his interests in order to develop time when you read together – make it a routine, daily activity where you sit down and share a book. This can be during free play, a structured work session, class reading or the Literacy Hour.

Chapter 4

Choose books with clear, bright pictures that you think the child might enjoy. If they are linked to his special interests, try to expand the field as much as possible. An interest in Postman Pat, for example, can be extended to books about postmen, cats, vans or other television characters.

Books with noises or flaps are good for young children and tactile books are sometimes popular and certainly easy to make if you have time. Remember, though, that some children with autistic spectrum disorders are sensitive to certain textures, although there may be others they particularly enjoy.

For a young child with poor communication skills, it is important to choose repetitive, simple stories and keep language at a level he can understand. At first, you may only manage to get through the book, turning one page at a time, and all you need to say is, 'Turn the page' in a repetitive, interesting manner. You may then be able to explore the book more fully by lifting flaps, feeling textures and pressing buttons to make sounds. Point to pictures that might be familiar (cat, meow!) and prompt the child to point to the picture and say the word.

Book bags or stories with props are helpful for all young children but particularly for those who have difficulty understanding the language and concept of a story. Stories can be prepared in advance and used daily until the child is ready to move on to another book. For example, a story about animals may come with assorted toy animals; the child learns to associate the pictures and the story with the animal by matching the correct animal to the picture in the book, the spoken word and the sound the animal makes.

For a child who is learning that written words have meaning, the book bag activity can be extended so that the child matches the written word to the toy or prop and the picture in the book.

Easier, but not quite so appealing, is to use a magnet board or felt board with pictures from the book to tell the story, making the pictures big and bright. When the child starts to recognise written words, he can match the words with the pictures on the board.

It is important when looking at a storybook together to keep language simple and not to start reading a story with complex sentences if the child does not have the language skills to understand.

Group stories can be made more accessible to children with language difficulties by using props, puppets and large pictures. To include a child with autism in a group story, give him a toy linked to the story, a sound or a choice he can make. For example, if you have a picture for each page, children in the class can take turns coming up and choosing the correct picture for that page to place on a magnetic board, felt board or piece of mounting card with strips of Velcro across it.

Books of photographs with a single word or a short sentence describing each picture, as well as storybooks about children, families and familiar communities, can be more meaningful to children with an autistic spectrum disorder than books in which animals dress in clothes, drive cars and talk to each other. The latter can be very difficult for some children to understand, although they will enjoy them if they have seen the characters in a video or film.

Books about characters the child particularly likes will be motivating but may need to be rewritten or retold in simple language. You could use the characters to make books to help a particular child read and enjoy stories if you have a child who is very difficult to motivate.

Poetry can become more accessible if it is accompanied by sounds or other sensory input, such as the sound of wind or a whisper. If you have a poem with a good punchline, dramatise it and leave a gap for a child to fill in. Some children with autism may need more repetition to understand and enjoy a poem, but if you have a good short poem with a dramatic punchline, why not include it at the end of every lesson? Other children will enjoy it too.

Children with autistic spectrum disorders who can read may do so without understanding what they are reading. You can help them understand that stories have meaning and are not just a series of words on a page by making books using photographs of themselves and their family or friends. Spend time each day talking about familiar scenes in pictures and photographs before moving on to short picture books depicting everyday situations.

Teaching children with autistic spectrum disorders to read

Some children with autistic spectrum disorders learn to sight-read easily. They do not understand the sounds the different letters and groups of letters make, but seem to have a precocious skill in knowing what the words are. This skill is called hyperlexia. If a child has hyperlexia, everyone will be impressed by his ability when other children are struggling to learn to read. However, it is important to help a child with an autistic spectrum disorder to not only read but understand what he is reading. He needs to be aware of not only the content and plot of the story but the meanings of different words and concepts.

Other children with autism have more difficulty learning to read. They may easily learn by rote the names and sounds of letters but be unable to understand that the sounds fit together to form a word. When they see a letter on the page, that is what they see; a letter name and a letter sound. They may appear to be learning to read because they know some storybooks off by heart, but then they fail to progress. They need a lot of help to understand that words have meanings and to see the whole word, not just the letters they have learnt.

In cases like these, it can be easier to use a multisensory approach and very motivating materials.

Words will be given meaning when they are attached to something that is meaningful to the child. You can start developing early reading skills by labelling items in the environment. At home you could label the fridge, television, video and different rooms. At school, many things are routinely labelled but make sure labels are attached to items of particular interest to the child – the computer or headphones, for example. Then, when he is making choices, he can choose from a board of written words instead of symbols and pictures. A first reading book can be made showing photographs of him at school using the things he enjoys.

If a child knows some books off by heart, photocopy the pictures, cut up the sentences and ask him to stick the sentences back in order and read them back to you. At first, this may be a simple matching exercise, finding the correct words and sticking them under the sentence, but, as the activity becomes more familiar, leave some gaps in the sentences so the child can fill the words in without the visual prompt.

Teach whole words, starting with familiar names, words in the environment and words in books the child already knows. It sometimes helps to make up cards with the word and symbol on one side and the word alone on the other. It is then more likely that the child will always be successful, which is very motivating. At the simplest level, you can make up a book of photographs of family members or favourite foods and teach the child to match the appropriate word or name with each photograph. Using Velcro, so he can stick the words under the pictures, can make this activity more interesting.

When a child can read some words and is gaining confidence, work on initial letter sounds. Using computer programs with pictures and symbols, as shown here, is a good way to teach initial sounds and has the added advantage of helping develop independent working skills.

At the Zoo

Fill in the missing letters on all the words

_ion   _iraffe   _nake

_ear   _iger   _angaroo

_amel   _lephant   _ippo

_onkey   _orilla   _eer

b c d e g h k l m s t

Using symbols to support literacy skills. *Symbols from Widget 2000*

Remind the child to look at the page and try to guess from the picture what a word may be. Because children with autism have difficulty doing two things at once and making a connection between them, they do not usually think about the picture when they are trying to read a sentence. They need to be prompted to do so.

Rewrite simple storybooks using a symbols computer program so the child has the symbols to help. As most children with autism are visual learners who 'think in pictures', this can give them confidence and help give meaning to the words. As the child gains confidence, you can start leaving some symbols off words that are repeated a lot or can be easily guessed from the context.

Children with autistic spectrum disorders have difficulty with imagination. They might find it easier to read stories they can easily relate to or non-fiction books about things that interest them.

Help children make their own books. Use computer graphics, photographs, pictures, drawings or concrete reminders of trips out and special activities. Encourage the child to talk about what is on the page and scribe for him if necessary. Use the child's own words, even if it is only one word. You can always put a more lengthy sentence underneath.

Reading and writing require sequencing skills. Many children with autistic spectrum disorders have difficulty sequencing. Very early skills can be taught by sequencing patterns – for example, building a tower or threading beads following a coloured sequencing guide. At first, the child matches the beads to the guide and threads them. Then, as he becomes more confident, he may have ten beads but the guide shows the pattern for eight beads, then six, then four until he is able to continue a pattern of three or four beads. It is possible to buy books with a variety of different picture sequences to arrange in order, using cutting and sticking or putting a ring around the next picture in the sequence.

Sequencing language activities can be practised by using sets of sequencing cards, retelling events and stories in the correct sequence, understanding phrases such as 'What happened before?' and 'What happened next?' Use photos of the child doing an activity – making a fruit salad or getting dressed, say – and sequence them to make a book. Take it step by step.

Helping children with handwriting difficulties

Children with autistic spectrum disorders often have difficulties with fine motor skills. They may not have enough control to hold the pencil and form a letter. Writing requires the physical skill of holding a pencil and forming a letter and the understanding that what they are doing has meaning. Either of these skills may be difficult for a child with autism.

Sometimes they learn to form some capital letters that are easy, such as A or O, and learn that that letter has a name. They receive a lot of praise from parents and teachers as they have begun to master an important skill. Then they copy the letter over and over and it is difficult to move them on.

Alternatively, they may learn to write numbers and cover a piece of paper with numbers and nothing else. It can be hard to move a child forward when writing the same thing becomes fixed and repetitive. A lack of imagination may mean the child does not understand that the graphics they are using have meaning and represent objects.

What you can do

Pencil skills
Start with early pencil skills. Can the child copy a straight line (horizontal, then vertical) or a circle? Can he draw a face or a person? Teach him to copy first a horizontal line, then a vertical line, then a circle. Use a physical prompt if necessary or share a large sheet of paper.

When the child is happy and confident using a pencil, show him how to hold it properly. It is important to do this because children with autism are very resistant to change so it will be very difficult to alter how they write if you do not start them on the right track when they are young. Here are some ideas.

- Use large sheets of paper and write on them with highlighter pen, creating thick lines the child can trace over.

- Use a white board, a flip chart or draw with chalk on a wall or on the ground.

- If the child holds his pen loosely and makes light marks that are difficult to see, give him fat, brightly coloured pens.

- Make cards with patterns for the child to trace over. Laminate them so he can write directly on the cards and you can wipe them clean. Use lines, simple shapes and spirals, depending on the ability of the child.

- Drawing half a face or half a shape that the child has to finish is good for developing pencil skills. You can start by drawing half on a large sheet of paper and show the child how to copy on his side of the paper. When he has the idea, you can make up laminated cards for him to finish.

Capitals and lower case
Children are sometimes taught to write in capitals at home. This may seem sensible because capitals are easier to form and children learn them more quickly. However, it is very difficult to teach a child to use lower-case letters once they have learnt to use capitals and writing in capitals is very slow. Do not teach a child to use capitals unless every other strategy has failed. Discuss it with staff first.

Cursive writing
Because some children with autistic spectrum disorders have such difficulty learning to write and are so resistant to change, it may be worth considering teaching cursive writing from the beginning.

Lines
Many children with autistic spectrum disorders need lines as a guide when they are writing. They have difficulty creating their own imaginary lines and sometimes their writing gets larger and larger and uneven.

Writing independently

Children may learn to trace or copy but have difficulty writing independently. When a child has learned to trace over his name confidently, leave off the last letter. If he does not fill it in, leave off the end of the last letter. Each time he writes his name leave off a little bit more. If necessary prompt him to complete his name, but try to do it lightly and withdraw the prompt next time.

Developing understanding of words

Teach words that are meaningful to the child. Children with autism will sit and copy over letters with no understanding of their meaning. They may find it hard to transfer the skill of forming letters along a line in a book to writing words that have meaning.

Teach words they can read that are linked to their interests. If a child wants you to write out the names of every tube station on the Northern Line, try leaving off the last letter of the last station. At first, you will have to prompt him to finish it and he will probably be upset but the next day will be easier. Gradually expect him to do more writing. It will develop his confidence and it will then be easier to find other ways of encouraging independent writing.

Overcoming fear of failure

Children with autistic spectrum disorders can become anxious about making mistakes. This sometimes prevents them doing any work unless they feel confident they can do it perfectly.

A social story (see page 83) can be helpful to reassure them that it is OK to make mistakes. You may find it easier to let them use an eraser initially, then gradually limit when they can use it. Maybe you could let them use it for tasks they will find difficult, but not for routine tasks.

Reference material

Children sometimes find it easier to write independently if they can see the alphabet on their book or table. They then have a visual reminder of what the letters look like.

Keyboard skills

Teach keyboard skills to children with autism who have writing difficulties. Make sure right from the beginning that they use both hands. They may start off typing with two fingers but they should use their left and right hands for the left and right sides of the keyboard.

Whatever difficulties a child with autism may have when developing his literacy skills, a consistent approach that combines repetition with creative use of the child's special interests to develop teaching materials is a good starting point. As the child gains confidence, new topics can be introduced, providing they follow small steps and do not demand too big a leap in understanding. It may seem at first that you have to spend a lot of time adapting materials for one child. However, you will find with practice that you can develop new materials quickly and there may be other children who can also benefit from your expertise.

Teaching an understanding of number

Children with autistic spectrum disorders are often very good at reciting and ordering numbers. Many recognise written numbers from one to ten at an early age and love to name them and line them up. They find it easy to learn by rote and may learn to count to large numbers but not understand a simple instruction like 'give me three biscuits', even when the instruction is given with a visual number three.

In order to move on and learn to use maths in daily routines, a child needs to have a firm grasp of basic number concepts. Real understanding of number may only come after a lot of practice of repetitive, practical activities.

What you can do

There are many opportunities throughout the day at home and school to teach an understanding of number. For example, counting eyes, ears, buttons on coats, steps, jumps, spoons, plates, biscuits, sweets, grapes, apples and so on. Although new concepts and structured activities are best taught at a quiet time when there are few distractions, number skills the child has learned should be supported by plenty of practical examples at home and school.

Matching

In the early stages, it can be helpful to have cards with a number on each and spaces drawn at the bottom as a simple matching exercise. The child then matches small objects to the spaces.

There are many wonderful resources to help children develop early number concepts but children with autism can find the colours and quantity of objects too overwhelming and many do not know what to do with it all. Similarly, many children learn and practise skills through play, but a child with autism will need guidance and prompting in order to do so. Simple information, clearly and visually presented with plenty of practical experience to support it, is best at this stage.

For example, you may be working on understanding numbers one and two. Make up number cards showing the numbers one and two – you will need these later. Now, make bigger cards with the numbers one and two on them with circles or squares underneath or a strip of Velcro. The child can then either match an object to the circles or squares or stick one or two pictures on the Velcro.

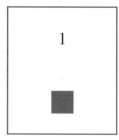
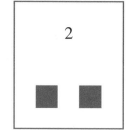

When a child can match the correct number of objects to the number on each card, use the smaller cards you made earlier without the squares. Hold one up, then ask the child to drop the matching number of objects in to a posting box (empty crisps tubes are good as they make a satisfying 'clunk' when the object drops in), thread the right number of beads or cotton reels on to a lace, put biscuits on to a plate, drop balls down the helter skelter or whatever other activity you choose.

When you have had plenty of practice with one and two, increase the numbers gradually to five, then ten.

Number songs

You can use number songs with pictures that are stuck to a board, added and counted as each verse is sung. Many number songs introduce numbers in diminishing order. It is best to adapt these songs and start at number one, increasing to number five.

For example, if you have 15 yellow ducks and a magnetic board you could sing *Five little ducks.*

Five little ducks
Five little ducks went swimming one day,
Over the hill and far away,
Mother duck said 'Quack, quack, quack',
But only one little duck came back.
(child puts one duck on the board)

Five little ducks went swimming one day,
Over the hill and far away,
Mother duck said 'Quack, quack, quack',
But only two little ducks came back
(child puts two ducks on the board)

... and so on to five.

Songs like this can be varied in many different ways. If you are teaching 'add one', the child can put one duck on the board each time and count the total as he goes. If you are teaching 'take away one', the child can start with five ducks on the board and take one off each time, counting how many ducks are left.

Interactive books

You could make an interactive book using laminated pages, with picture and number cards attached with Velcro. The ducks can then be removed and counted, added or subtracted on each page, depending what you are working on at the time.

Using Writing with symbols 2000'

If a child has special interests, you may be able to use that to help develop an understanding of number. If he likes trains, for example, you could do some work with trains, carriages, signals, drivers and so on. You could make a number line with a train and numbered carriages or make a book and ask him to put a certain number of people in each carriage. If you have access to a digital camera, you could make the book more interesting by using photos of family members or other children in the class. If you do make a book and you want the child to match a number on each page with a number of objects or people, it can be helpful to put all the numbers and all the pictures on Velcro. Then, when the child has learnt the numbers in order, you can jumble them up and teach them in a different order.

Increasing understanding

When a child has counted a number of objects arranged in a line (for example, small cubes), jumble them up and ask him to count them again while they are spread out on the table. Many children with autistic spectrum disorders have difficulty doing this and it can help to provide a pot or tub to count the objects in to.

Stamping activities

Stamps and a stamp pad can be good fun to use for counting activities.

You can give a child a piece of paper with a number on it and ask him, for example, to 'stamp four cats'. When he has more understanding and can work independently, he can go down a page of numbers, stamping the correct number of pictures beside each one.

As a variation, draw or cut and stick the correct number of objects beside each number. Link the pictures used to favourite stories or interests.

Using dice

Play dice games so the child learns to recognise numbers up to six without counting the dots each time.

One easy game to play uses a dice, counters and a board of squares for each player. The child throws the dice and covers the correct number of squares with counters. The first person to cover all their squares is the winner. Some children may need to practise with an adult first, but, when they are confident, ask another child to play, too.

Beginning to add

Many children with autistic spectrum disorders can count up to ten but become confused when shown how to add and, in particular, how to use a number line. One reason for this may be that they have not developed a concept of number and need to practise some of the ideas given above. When you are sure the child does have a concept of number, you can practise adding on.

Start adding on using practical examples. Do not introduce paper and pencil until you are sure the child is ready. Looking at numbers and writing an answer is an additional skill, so give a good grounding using practical examples first.

After counting a set of objects, ask the child what the total would be if he added 'one more'.

Use the same phrase until you are sure the child understands it. Then introduce new vocabulary gradually. Children with autism are inflexible in their thinking and have difficulty generalising what they have learnt from one example to another. Every time they learn a new way to do the same thing, it can be like starting again, so take it slowly, step by step, and use plenty of visual examples.

- Use your fingers and ask the child to count how many fingers you are holding up.

- Use large dice with dots. Throw two dice and ask the child to count the number of dots on the tops of the dice. If he recognises the number of dots on one dice he can count on from that number. Alternatively, use one dice with numbers and one with dots. Throw them both and ask the child to count on from the number dice. Similarly, you can use dominoes instead of dice.

- Before introducing a number line, teach the child to count on using a simple game board with ten blank squares and a large dice with numbers on the faces. Two children could play if they both had their own board.

When the child is confident counting along the squares, number the squares and use two dice with dots totalling no more than ten. The child counts the dots on the first dice, finds that number and puts his counter on it. He then counts the number on the second dice and counts on. You can put an additional Velcro strip at the bottom of the board and a set of numbers so the child can see the corresponding number at each stage of the process. When he is confident with this, try introducing a number line.

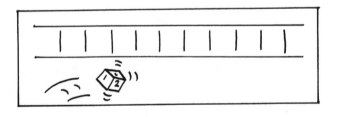

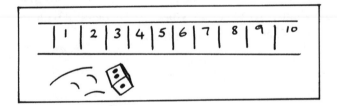

Some children are very good at mental maths. For those who find it difficult, teach them a visual strategy. Put your hand on your head to remember the number. If they still have difficulty, using fingers to aid early adding and subtracting can be more positive than not succeeding at all. Using fingers to add can also help children who struggle with maths and are very dependent on using small cubes – they have the added advantages of always being available and portable!

It is helpful to put an emphasis on mathematical concepts such as 'more', 'less', 'all', 'some', 'before' and 'after' at an early stage. These concepts can be difficult to grasp for children with language difficulties and an inability to think flexibly or generalise information across a range of examples. Likewise, estimation, rounding up and rounding down may also need to be taught with many examples and much repetition.

Developing social interaction skills

Children with autistic spectrum disorders have difficulty understanding and interacting with others. They may be aloof or eccentric, run around with the other children in the playground but not interact with them, be confused by social overtures and have difficulty expressing themselves. Children who have sensory difficulties will also find the noise, movement and proximity of others in the playground and classroom hard to cope with.

What you can do

Learning to share
With young children in nursery, you need to set up situations where the child learns to share and take turns. Turn-taking activities have been covered more fully in Chapter 1 as it is also an important early communication skill.

Start by playing games where you take turns. Say 'My turn, your turn... .' When the child accepts taking turns with an adult, invite another child to join in. Say 'My turn, your turn, Johnnie's turn.'

In this way, the child learns to understand that his turn will come and the toy he wants so much has not gone forever.

Teach the child to 'wait'
This is an important social skill that helps a child to take turns and share without becoming distressed. For more on this subject, see page 42.

Model play skills
Show the child how to play and, when he is confident in a certain play routine, invite other children to join in.

Awareness of others
If a child walks over other children on the carpet without realising that they are there, try giving him his own place to sit on the carpet. Make this near the edge so he can get out easily.

Also, show him how to step over other children. If his language skills are good, teach him to say 'Excuse me' and write a social story with photographs about saying 'Excuse me.'

Chapter 6

Social interaction tasks

Teach the child how to do tasks that involve social interaction. For example, show him how to go to the office with another child to get the register, give out the milk, choose the story from a choice of two or three at storytime and so on.

If you have times when you sing in the nursery, have a picture for each song pinned to a board and invite the children to choose one. If you are telling a story to a group of children, include an element of choice or an action that a child with autism can do to join in.

Buddies

Implementing a buddy system for the playground can be very beneficial.

Buddies can be children as young as four or five, providing they are told what to do and when to get adult help. Buddies can wear buddy badges and feel special for the day. It is important to ask for volunteers to be a buddy every day as, otherwise, it may fall too much to one or two children.

Buddy Badge

buddy

A buddy system can also be reassuring for parents who can be worried that their child will be bullied in a large playground.

If two buddies are chosen every day, they find it easier than an adult to stay with the child as he moves around the playground and it is much better for a child to be supported by his peers. Buddies may also be children from older classes, providing they are given clear guidelines for what is expected and when to seek adult help.

Discuss social matters

Talk to all the children about helping each other. Young children may be egocentric but they can understand why some children need extra support.

Utilise classroom assistants

If a child has adult support, use that to enable him to join in group activities. It is easy to find yourself creating a situation in which the child is interacting all the time with the adult separate from the rest of the class.

Make the most of circle time

Use circle time to encourage children to take turns and listen to others.

You can make this explicit by having an object that each child holds when it is his or her turn to speak. This can be developed further in a small group by checking that the children are listening to each other. You could do this subtly by pretending that you did not hear and ask the child holding the object what the previous child said.

Set up a lunchtime club

The club can make organised games and activities available so that children who need extra help with social interaction and play skills can have support. Each child can invite a friend and it can be a special time to teach new social and play skills.

Lunchtime clubs can also focus on children's special interests, maybe once a week. Younger children could have a Thomas the Tank Engine club or a dinosaur club and older children could have a computer club. Whatever the subject, it is an opportunity for the child with autism to be with others who share his interests and hobbies.

Circle of friends

'Circle of friends' is an idea that originated in the USA to help support the inclusion of children with additional educational needs in mainstream schools.

It is an effective technique that uses peer support to help children who are having difficulties with social interaction, independence skills and learning. It is most suitable for children in Key Stage 2 and older, although a younger child could have a circle of friends if there was plenty of adult support available at the beginning.

A circle of friends is usually a group of eight children, with the focus child, supported by an adult. The group meets weekly for 20 to 30 minutes for the first 10 weeks, then decides whether to carry on meeting this regularly or less frequently.

The idea behind the circle of friends is that the peer group makes decisions and works out strategies that will help the focus child with difficulties he may be having.

Example 1

Luke is a quiet year 4 boy who has only recently been diagnosed with autism. He has always been to a mainstream school and received adult support.

He has coped fairly well with a differentiated curriculum, but, at playtime, until he had a circle of friends, he was either on his own or played with much younger children. He had started hitting out at other children on the stairs or at other unstructured times during the day and was not able to express his feelings, even to adults he knew well.

At his first annual review following his diagnosis of autism, the specialist teacher for children with autistic spectrum disorders discussed the possibility of having a circle of friends with Luke's parents. They liked the idea and, when it was discussed with Luke, he thought it sounded good and that it would help him.

The specialist teacher volunteered to come in to talk to the class and run the circle for ten weeks with the learning support assistant, who was able to feed back what had been happening during the week. During the class talk, Luke was taken out to the library to work.

The class was told what a circle of friends was for and how it would work. The pupils were encouraged to think about things they found difficult and how they would feel if they had difficulty making friends. They were then asked to think about the things that Luke was good at and a list was drawn up. A list was also drawn up of the things he found difficult.

The teacher suggested that friends can help with things that are difficult and that a circle of friends could help Luke and make him feel happier at school. The children were told that they would have to give up one lunchtime play every week and were then asked to volunteer. Many more than eight children volunteered, so the teacher chose a group he felt would be most supportive. Everyone was reminded to support the circle of friends, even if they had not volunteered or been chosen.

Luke's parents' permission was sought and, once all the permission slips were in, the circle began. It met one lunchtime a week and began by looking again at Luke's strengths and the things he found difficult – this time with him contributing.

Some things were targeted and strategies agreed on. In particular, the friends agreed to help Luke in the playground by teaching him games and making sure he was included.

The circle started off well, but by the fourth week there were serious difficulties. The two girls were finding that they had all the responsibility for supporting Luke at playtime and one girl dropped out. Her brother had autism and she found that playing a supporting role at school as well as at home was too much for her. The boys wanted to play football all the time and Luke was slow and clumsy, with no ball skills. Everyone, apart from Luke, felt that they did not want to give up a lunchtime play every week. They tried to disappear out of the classroom before the circle of friends meeting began. Only Luke was happy with the circle of friends. He felt he had friends and his self-esteem was growing week by week.

The learning support assistant and the teacher encouraged each child in the circle to say what was going well and what was going badly. They were asked to think of what they could do about the bad things and each child gave an opinion or made a suggestion. They decided to take turns every day to support Luke in the playground and to try some new games that other children might enjoy. They also decided to ask the teacher to speak to the class, reminding them to support the circle of friends and find another girl to join the circle.

Two girls joined the circle and the rota system worked so well that, after a few weeks, it was tacitly dropped.

At the end of the ten weeks, the members of the circle were asked to say what they thought about how it had gone. They all felt positive about it and wanted it to continue. They suggested a posting box where they could write down things they needed to talk about with the learning support assistant or class teacher.

A year on, Luke is so much more confident that he seems a different boy. He is able to speak out in a stronger voice and give his opinion about things. He feels he has friends and knows where to turn when he is having difficulties or is unhappy.

A circle of friends rarely runs smoothly from beginning to end. However, sorting out difficulties in a structured group with adult support is a very positive experience for children. In some ways it is better if the circle of friends is not run by the class teacher as then the children may feel more able to speak out and say what they really think. The important thing is that they work things through themselves and take credit for their success.

Social Stories

Social stories were developed in the USA by Carol Gray (see References, page 103). If they are constructed properly, they can work wonderfully for children who are having difficulties understanding social situations and managing to cope with change.

They work best for children who have the ability to understand simple sentences, but they can also be presented in pictures, symbols or with photographs to help younger or less able children understand what to do in certain social situations or to reassure them that what is happening is going to be OK.

For example, when children are moving up to reception from nursery, they could have a social story to prepare them for the change. The story could be in book form with photographs showing the new classroom, the new teacher and the things that will still be the same – the children, the learning support assistant, the work bay for individual work and so on.

Carol Gray describes the three main types of sentences that are to be found in her social stories. These are:

- **descriptive** describing what is happening or what will happen and why
- **perspective** describing how people feel and react to certain situations
- **directive** describing what should happen in a given situation.

Carol Gray's stories are descriptive and have perspective. A short story will have one directive statement only. She uses phrases such as 'usually' and 'I will try to ...' in order to avoid making statements that leave no room for error or exceptions. This is because children with autistic spectrum disorders will often take what is said very literally and find it hard to accept changes to rules.

Carol Gray has edited books of social stories that are a good starting point if you want to start writing your own stories for particular children and situations. They can be adapted and give a good feel of what to write and what works well.

Example 2
Jack was coping very well in his mainstream primary school and his literacy skills were developing well. However, he lacked the confidence to work independently because he was always worried that he would make an error and erasers were not allowed in the classroom.

Even when an exception was made for him, Jack could not relax because he knew that, by using an eraser, he was breaking a class rule.

Adults working with him decided to try a social story, which he read before he started his written work and it was then placed where he could easily see it. This is what it said:

Sometimes when I am writing I make a mistake.
Sometimes other children in my class make mistakes.

Mrs Brown tells us to put a cross through the mistake.
I will try to put a cross through my mistakes and carry on with my work.
Mrs Brown will be pleased that I have finished my work by myself.
She will give me a special sticker when I cross out my mistakes and finish
my work.

Within three weeks, Jack was able to do his writing and cross out his mistakes
without anxiety.

Lack of imagination and flexible thought

Children with autistic spectrum disorders have difficulty with imagination and flexible thinking. This will present itself in a number of different ways but in younger children it particularly affects the way they play. Young children learn through play and it is more difficult for them to learn and socialise with their peers if they do not play and are not able to think imaginatively and flexibly.

They also have difficulty generalising what they have learnt across a range of settings and become confused if a task or routine they know well is changed or presented in a different way.

They may have good language skills but take everything literally. When they are told to 'go and get in the bath', for example, they may do just that, but do not take off their clothes or run the water.

They are often resistant to change and can become very distressed if the daily routine changes or new displays are put up on the classroom walls.

The following examples are just some of the strategies that can be tried to help young children become more flexible and imaginative. However, although it is possible to teach play routines and help children to make choices and manage change, the inflexibility of a child with an autistic spectrum disorder is a difficult aspect to alter. As stressed throughout this book, it is important to be aware of the difficulties, teach skills in small steps using visual prompts, have clear targets and be creative when looking for solutions.

> *Example 1*
> John manipulates the wheels of a toy but does not play with it imaginatively.

Target
John will play 'pretend' games with cars, trains and other toys.

Strategies
- Teach play skills by modelling what he can do with different toys.
- If possible, have two identical toys and encourage him to copy you.
- Use toys that capture his interest, such as noisy puppets, big sunglasses, floppy hats, squeaky teddies, cars with lights and sirens, balls with bells inside and so on.
- Teach pretend play using the home corner, construction equipment, 'small world' toys.

- Take everything step by step and use a lot of repetition and prompting.
- When he has learnt a play routine, invite another child to join in.
- If John enjoys watching videos, try showing a video of some children playing with a particular toy (cars on a car mat, train and train track, construction) and provide John with the same toys to encourage him to copy.

Example 2
Josie does not play imaginative games with her peers but will play solitary games based on video or storybook characters.

Target
Josie will join in a class game based on a story theme.

Strategies
- Use drama and group games to develop new ideas. For example, develop a theme over several days linked to a story or a particular topic. Have a clear target and work on it in small steps, such as 'Josie will pretend to be on a boat in a storm.'
- Use simple props – eye patches for pirates and large construction for the boat with music, wind, rocking waves and other special effects, for example.
- Use modelling, prompting and repetition to show Josie what to do.

Example 3
Joshua insists that games are played in certain ways and becomes distressed if somebody tries to change them.

Target
Joshua will accept other children joining in and changing the rules or storyline of his games.

Strategies
- Join in the game and make very subtle changes at first. Do this by breaking it down in to very small steps, such as:
  - Joshua will allow an adult to take a turn with his fire engine
  - Joshua will interact with an adult when playing with his fire engine
  - Joshua will follow an adult's ideas and let her follow his when playing with his fire engine
  - Joshua will allow another child to join him when he is playing with an adult.
- Keep persevering with this until Joshua accepts more flexibility with his game.
- Teach Joshua new games in structured settings, then generalise them to classroom and playground settings.
- Use a social story to explain how children play games and add their own ideas.

Example 4
Jamie will be upset for the whole day if his routine is changed.

Target
Jamie will accept changes to his daily routine.

Strategies

- Write a social story to prepare Jamie for changes in advance – for example, what will happen when his teacher is away.
- Prepare him for big changes, such as moving to a new class, by having a transition plan. This may include a social story with photographs and visits to the new class.
- Use a timetable and change it immediately there are any alterations.
- Use a consistent substitute for a cancelled favourite activity (swimming, for example).
- Try to avoid unnecessary changes.

Example 5
George is obsessed with his collection of dinosaurs and does not want to put them down when he comes into the classroom. He writes about dinosaurs and always insists on having a dinosaur somewhere in all his drawings.

Target
George will only play with three dinosaurs when he has finished his work.

Strategies

- Implement a rule that George is only allowed to bring three dinosaurs into class. This will be hard for his family, so gradually decrease the number of dinosaurs by allowing one less every week. A visual chart showing this may help George.
- Write a social story telling George when he can have his dinosaurs or talk and write about them.
- Reduce anxiety for George at school by providing a structure with visual guidance.
- Use the dinosaurs as a reward for completing work. Show on his timetable when he is allowed to play, talk or write about them.
- Let George have a special dinosaur project where he has to find out broader things about dinosaurs, such as what the world was like then, how they looked after their babies and so on.
- Dinosaurs can be used to help George with things he finds difficult – adding and subtracting, classifying and sorting, for example. However, these are not George's dinosaurs so, if he finds them distracting and inaccurate, use something else.

Example 6
Shereen has difficulty writing about fictional characters or telling stories unless they are based on her favourite videos.

Target
Shereen will write simple stories that are not based on videos.

Strategies

- Use puppets, dressing-up items, simple props and role play to encourage imaginative play and new ideas.
- Start by sequencing photographs of something Shereen has done – for example, a role play, dressing-up game, day out, cooking or art activity. Write a caption for each page and make it into a book.
- Retell a familiar story using the pictures in the book as a guide.
- Retell a familiar story and ask Shereen to draw her own pictures to make a book.

- Talk about a single picture, about why something happened, what happened before and what might happen next. Use drawings and speech bubbles to help plan out the story sequence.
- Build the single picture into a story by asking Shereen to draw before and after pictures and write an accompanying story.
- Use other prompts – objects , situations, other stories and so on.

Example 7
Michael takes language literally and will sometimes misunderstand what is said or feel threatened by it.

Target
Michael will learn the meanings of common sayings and idioms.

Strategies
- Adults working with Michael should be aware of what they are saying and check that Michael has understood what has been said.
- Teach the meaning of common ambiguous sayings, such as 'that was a tongue-twister', using drawings and discussion.

"That's a tongue twister!"

Theory of mind

In 1995, S. Baron-Cohen argued that one cause of autistic spectrum disorders may be a failure of the individual to develop a 'Theory of Mind'. Research has shown that children with autism have great difficulty taking others' thoughts into account and may not be aware that you have your own thoughts and needs. They may also believe you know what they are thinking, so they will start a conversation with no reference to what the conversation is about. They have difficulty showing empathy with others, expressing their own feelings or predicting from non-verbal cues or previous experience what will happen in a social situation. This sometimes results in finding others' behaviour confusing or frightening, causing anxiety, fear and sudden aggressive or unexpected behaviour.

What you can do

- Make your meaning clear and do not assume that a child with an autistic spectrum disorder knows what you mean by your facial expression, gestures or tone of voice.
- Try to be calm and keep your voice calm in the classroom.
- If possible, give the child his own quiet corner where he can work if he is having difficulty coping in a group.
- Try different things that may be calming, such as listening to music through headphones.
- Organise the child's support so there is help at unstructured times of the day.
- Give him a routine activity at transition times so he knows exactly what to do.

Examples of Symbols used to talk about feelings

• Use stories, photos, drawings and real situations to talk about feelings. Start with simple, familiar feelings, such as happy, sad, angry, scared.

• Use toys and puppets to model feelings or responses to feelings.

• If there is an incident in the playground, classroom or at home, draw pictures to help the child talk about it and how different individuals might be feeling.

• Children who find it hard to express their feelings might be able to do so if you write down what they say (or type it on a screen) and write down their response without looking at them directly. They are then focused on what you are saying and are more able to follow the conversation because they can read it on the page and do not need to hold it in their heads.

It can be difficult to help children with autistic spectrum disorders develop social understanding and generally it is best to use real situations to explore meanings and emotions and to reflect on what has happened. If a child does have the communication skills to explain an event, or a photograph of an event from his perspective, you may be surprised how his interpretation of what has happened differs from yours. You can learn a great deal from this and use it as a starting point to help the child become less confused in social situations.

For children who do not have the communication skills you can use mime, modelling and shaping behaviour to teach a more correct response.

Lack of imagination
and flexible thought

Behaviour support strategies

When working with or caring for children with autistic spectrum disorders, it is important to remember that the behaviour you find difficult to manage is a reflection of difficulties they are experiencing because they have autism (you will recall the triad of impairments described at the beginning of the book).

The most important first step when looking for strategies is to work out the reasons behind the behaviour and to try to understand it from the child's point of view. For example, many parents say that the most difficult behaviour of their young children (tantrums, aggression, refusal to comply with requests) seems to be due to the child's lack of communication skills. One of the positive effects of using PECS (see page 37) to develop communication skills is that it reduces frustration and gives the child some control over his environment.

There are many reasons for children with autism doing and saying things that we find challenging or eccentric. If it is not clear what the cause is, it can be helpful to record the following information:

• when the behaviour occurs and who is present at the time
• what happened immediately before the incident
• description of the incident
• what happened afterwards.

A pattern may emerge that should give some idea of what is causing the behaviour and then strategies can be put in place to try and put it right. Sometimes, there are several reasons and these can be difficult to disentangle. However, more often there is one main reason that becomes obvious as a result of analysis and can provide a starting point. There are several other important points to keep in mind when you want to change a child's behaviour.

• **Be positive** Use rewards for acceptable behaviour rather than sanctions for unacceptable behaviour.
• **Be patient** Whatever strategy you decide to follow will not work immediately. Wait at least four weeks, particularly with a very young child, before deciding to try something else. Some strategies, such as developing a method of communication, are very long term, especially with children who have additional learning needs.
• **Be consistent** Make sure that everybody who spends time with the child knows how to respond to the target behaviour and sticks to the strategy.
• **Be calm** An angry or loud response might help you feel better, but it is unlikely to help the child.
• **Be creative** Do not be afraid to try new ideas if you think they might work.

Some strategies are difficult to put into practice in mainstream schools. These include food rewards, access to the playground, ignoring screaming or other noises, providing a quiet, calm environment. Flexibility, staff training for all staff, co-operative work with parents and other professionals and a willingness to make inclusion work are all important factors in helping a child with an autistic spectrum disorder succeed in school.

Behaviour support strategies: some examples

Example 1

Tolu has been in nursery for six weeks and has no extra support, although an application has been made for a statutory assessment.

He has limited vocabulary and does not interact with the other children. If they come near him or try to join in with what he is doing, he pushes them out of his way.

Possible reasons

• Other children are unpredictable and Tolu finds them frightening.
• Tolu does not know how to play or interact with his peers.
• Tolu does not understand that when he gives another child a turn, he will have a turn himself later.

Strategies

• Teach Tolu to take turns with an adult (see page 24).
• Teach Tolu to wait using a wait card (see page 42).
• For big things, such as taking turns on the trike, use a timer so that Tolu knows when it is time to change.
• Try to get extra support for Tolu so that he can be taught to play with his peers.
• If Tolu hurts another child, say calmly, 'No pushing. Be gentle' and show him what 'gentle' means by stroking his hand lightly.
• Keep trying the strategies regularly. It will take time for Tolu to change his behaviour.

Example 2

Amber is three and has been at playgroup for six weeks. She has severe communication difficulties but, given extra adult support, has begun to use a variety of materials and equipment.

However, Amber likes to throw toys in the air. This is dangerous and the toys often hit other children or knock things over.

Possible reasons

• Amber does not understand that she may hurt someone or what that means for the other child.
• She has no sense of safety, for herself or for others.
• She does not know how to play, interact or communicate with others.
• She may find the noise and activity around her makes her feel uncomfortable and throwing a toy calms her.

Strategies

• When Amber is throwing toys, pick them up and show her how to play with them. If it is a doll, for example, say 'no throwing, cuddle dolly' and model the behaviour you want for her.

- Teach Amber to throw a small beanbag or soft ball to an adult as a turn-taking game, then invite other children to join in.
- Teach Amber play skills by having an adult modelling and prompting play routines, then invite another child to join in.
- If Amber keeps throwing toys, take them away and take her to sit on a quiet chair for a minute. Then distract her to another activity.
- Try to provide some structure to Amber's time at playgroup by having a structured play session with an adult, outside playtime, relaxation time, storytime, drink and snack time. Have a visual timetable using symbols.

Example 3

Suzie has moved up to reception from nursery.

She has settled in well but will not use the toilet, even when it is clear that she wants to go. The toilets are used by several classes and are bigger and busier than the little toilets in the nursery.

Suzie will use the nursery toilet but, when she is taken back to the nursery, she wants to stay there and becomes so distressed it is hard to move her on to anything else.

Possible reasons

- Suzie is upset by the change of class and is unable to use the bigger toilets.
- Suzie does not like the smell or sounds in the bigger toilets – for example, there is a hot air dryer that is very noisy.
- It is a ploy to go back to the nursery.

Strategies

- It is common for children with autistic spectrum disorders to find the sound of hot air dryers and flushing toilets very frightening. Take Suzie to the staff toilet at a quiet time and see if she will go there.

- Take Suzie to visit the girls' toilets regularly twice a day when it is quiet, but do not ask her to use the toilet. Look at what is there or wash her hands if she will allow this.

Build up the time spent gradually and, when she seems confident, encourage her to use the toilet.
- Have a time to go to the toilet built in to her timetable.
- Set a time for Suzie to visit the nursery and put it on her timetable so that she knows she can still visit and when she can do so.
- Reward Suzie when she uses the toilet.

> *Example 4*
> Gurdeep is in the reception class. She has limited vocabulary and has a helper all the time. When she goes to PE, she runs very fast around the hall and does not follow instructions.

Possible reasons
- The hall is large and echoes and Gurdeep has difficulty understanding and following instructions.
- The hall has no structure and no boundaries, so Gurdeep does not know how to structure her time when she is in it.
- Gurdeep finds it is exciting to run around.
- Gurdeep does not understand the games and activities the class are asked to do in PE.

Strategies
- Have a mat that is Gurdeep's place. When the children are told to find a space, take her to her mat.
- Use gestures to help Gurdeep understand what she has to do.
- Practise sitting in the hall. Tell her to 'sit first, then run.'
- Give her a lot of praise for good responses.
- Hold her to give her a physical boundary when the children are sitting on the floor.
- Model for her what she should do and use physical and verbal prompts to help her.
- Increase expectations one step at a time.

> *Example 5*
> Joe is in the reception class. He has a helper from 9.30 am until 2.30 pm and works well with her in the morning.
>
> In the afternoon, though, he does not co-operate and frequently loses his temper, hitting anybody who comes near. His behaviour is unpredictable and there is a real concern that somebody will be badly hurt, so he is frequently sent home at 2.30 when his helper goes.

Possible reasons
- Joe does not like the school dinners. The school is trying to encourage healthy eating and does not allow children to bring a packed lunch. Consequently, Joe does not eat lunch.
- The afternoon is less structured and noisier than the morning and children do more play-based activities, such as construction, sand and water play. Joe may be sensitive to the sound and lack of structure in the classroom.
- Joe is very active and may be feeling tired by the afternoon.

Strategies
- Make sure that Joe has something he likes at lunchtime, even if it is brought from home.

Children with autism do not like change and are also sensitive to some smells and textures of food. He can be gradually encouraged to eat a wider diet after he has settled down at school.

- When the children are doing less structured activities, Joe could be taken out or to a quiet corner of the classroom to do a structured TEACCH session where he could practise skills he knows well with adult support.
- Children with autistic spectrum disorders lack imaginative skills and have difficulty developing play ideas and playing with others. He should practise these skills with an adult, then with one or two other children.
- Find a relaxing activity for Joe to do at the end of the day, after his helper has gone, or rearrange the helper's hours so that he has less time when he is unsupported at the end of the day.

Example 6
Lily is in the reception class. She likes playing in the sand but she always throws it up so that it blows in children's eyes and hair. Usually she is told off when this happens and taken away from the sand.

Possible reasons
- Lily likes to watch the sand as it falls down in a fine shower.
- She enjoys the fuss she creates when the sand goes in children's eyes.
- Throwing the sand is relaxing to Lily and it distracts her from the noisy play environment.
- Having limited play skills, Lily is pleased she has found something she enjoys.

Strategies
- Write a social story and read it to Lily before play.
- Use a very motivating reward when Lily does not throw sand.
- Say 'No throwing' and take her away from the sand without giving attention when she does throw some.
- Spend time teaching Lily how to play with other equipment and toys in the playground.

Example 7
Shenelle is in the reception class. She has good language skills and, when the children are on the carpet, she always calls out the answer without raising her hand. She also makes comments in a loud voice that are not relevant to the lesson.

Possible reasons
- Shenelle does not remember that she always has to raise her hand and wait to be asked the answer. It confuses here when she is not always chosen every time she raises her hand.
- Shenelle does not understand the social context of having a conversation, so she will say what she wants when it comes into her head.

Strategies
- Write a social story for Shenelle about what happens when the children are sitting on the carpet and what she should do.
- Have a reward system for Shenelle so that she can earn a reward when she has managed not to call out on the carpet. The reward could be something she enjoys, such as using the computer for five minutes.

- Have a visual notice using drawings on the wall near the teacher reminding children to raise their hands and wait their turn to be chosen. If Shenelle speaks out, point to the notice and say, 'Raise your hand and wait to be chosen.'
- Teach Shenelle turn-taking and waiting games.

Example 8
Adam is in year 1. He is obsessed with flags and can name and draw the flags of most countries in the world. However, he will not talk about anything else and will often talk about flags when he is supposed to be working.

Possible reasons
- Talking about flags makes Adam feel calm.
- He does not understand that flags are not interesting to others.
- He does not have social conversation skills and cannot join in the chat that happens between his peers.

Strategies
- Give Adam a written schedule for the day. Have the times that he is allowed to talk about flags written in it. Use it as a reward for finishing his work.
- Write a social story explaining when Adam can talk about flags.
- Use a timer so that Adam knows how long he has to talk about flags.
- Be firm with Adam and remind him when it is the wrong time to talk about flags – 'Work first, then flags'.
- Use flags to teach Adam things he may find difficult, such as maths, or to teach him other things about the countries they are from.
- Play games with Adam that will encourage him to listen to others. For example, try a conversation game where each child is given the first line and they have to take turns to keep the conversation going. Alternatively, use circle time to check that the children are listening to each other by choosing a child and asking what was just said.

Example 9
Jamie is in year 1. He is coping well academically but hates getting wet. If this happens when he is washing his hands or he splashes in a puddle, he will pull all his clothes off, wherever he is, and run about with no clothes on. He is also sensitive to certain textures on his skin and so refuses to wear waterproof aprons or overalls.

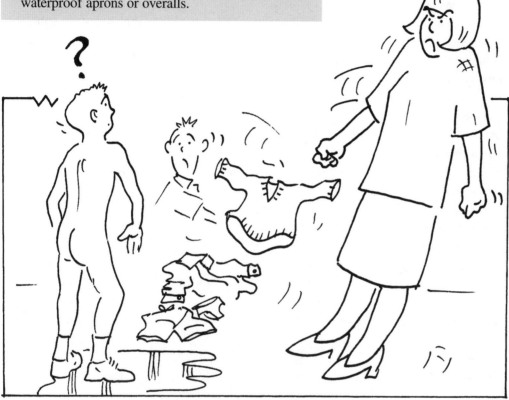

Possible reasons
• Jamie does not understand that it is not acceptable to run about naked.
• He is hypersensitive to the touch of wet clothing and cannot stand it near his skin.
• He does not know what to do when he gets wet.

Strategies
• Talk to Jamie's peers about what they can do to help Jamie – fetch an adult, take Jamie in to the toilets and so on.
• Write a social story for Jamie, telling him what to do if he gets wet.
• Teach Jamie how to change his wet clothes using the TEACCH method (see page 53) Keep a basket of clothes for Jamie in the toilets or some other suitable place where he can reach them. Teach him what to do by wetting his clothes and showing him how to change them.
• Have a buddy for Jamie who knows what to do and can support him if it happens.
• Build up Jamie's resistance to coping with wet clothing by dampening his clothes a little bit and having him wait before being able to change them. Try distraction, very motivating rewards, lots of praise, using a wait card and so on. Do this regularly and build up the time that he has to wait.

Example 10
Belle is in year 2. She has recently been diagnosed with Asperger syndrome. She is very tactless and upsets other children so they do not want to play with her. She takes what she wants without asking, so, for example, if she wants a pencil, she will snatch it from another child's hand. Recently she was found crying in the playground because she had no friends to play with.

Possible reasons
- Belle lacks social understanding and social interaction skills. She cannot imagine how other children feel when she upsets them.
- Belle may not know what to do in the playground and may feel lost and confused in an unstructured setting.

Strategies
- Write a social story about how to act in certain situations. What Belle should do when she is in a group sharing one pot of pencils would be one example.
- Set up a lunchtime club with other children who need extra help at playtime and teach playground games, board games and so on.
- Set up a circle of friends for Belle (see page 81).
- Do some work with Belle on understanding emotions using picture cards, photographs and real situations.
- Use 'Why? Because' cards (see Useful resources, page 107) to help Belle understand social situations. For example, talk about what is happening in a picture and try to think what might have happened before and why, then what will happen after and why. Use art, drama and role play to explore feelings and how to behave in social situations.

Example 11
Harry is in year 2. He has attention deficit hyperactivity disorder and autism. He has always gone home at lunchtime because he has difficulty coping in the unstructured, noisy playground.

The school has set up a lunchtime club for Harry and a group of other children who have difficulties with social interaction. However, when Harry was taken into the dining room, he attacked other children and threw his food on the floor.

Possible reasons
- Harry finds the dining room too noisy and there is too much activity. He feels afraid and panics.
- Harry did not understand that he was going to stay at school for dinnertime and is confused.
- Harry is having difficulty accepting the change to his routine.

Strategies
- Write a social story about what happens in the dining room at dinnertime and read it to Harry before dinner.
- Show Harry on his timetable that he is having dinner at school.
- Harry might cope better having his dinner at a table in a quiet area outside the dining area. When he can manage this calmly, gradually move the table nearer to the dining room. When he can manage sitting inside the door of the dining room, ask him to choose

a friend to sit beside him. Then join his table together with another table. This process may take several weeks and should be worked through at a pace that suits the child.

Example 12
Amy is in year 2. She has full-time support and her timetable is differentiated to meet her needs.

She has poor language skills and sometimes screams or cries and refuses to work. This disrupts the class and disturbs the teacher. She has to be taken out of the class when this happens, but there is nowhere to go but the playground or passageway.

Possible reasons
• Amy uses screaming to avoid working.
• She is confused about what she has to do and does not know how to ask for help.
• Suffering 'sensory overload', she needs to leave the room.
• Amy actually enjoys the attention she gets by screaming.

Strategies
• Use a visual timetable and structure Amy's work, showing her that when she has finished she can go outside to run around.
• Use a visual 'quiet' symbol to remind her not to make a noise.
• Try taking her to wash her hands or walk to the office then back to the classroom to do some more work.
• Present the tasks she has to do in a clear, visual way so that she is not confused by too much information (see Structured teaching, page 53).
• Offer positive, motivating rewards for finishing work.
• When she is taken out, always bring her back to the unfinished work, even if you have to finish it more quickly.
• Avoid giving attention to the screaming. Do not talk to her or make a fuss about it.
• Teach her relaxation using modelling and a visual social story.

quiet

Although behaviour support strategies may take days or weeks to succeed, it is important to be consistent as much as possible and ensure that everyone working with or caring for the child knows what the agreed response to certain behaviour should be. Parents, carers and school staff have to work together or the child will become confused and the behaviour you are trying to change could get worse. It is also worth remembering that if a child is used to getting attention by screaming, for example, and you withdraw that attention, the immediate response from the child will be to scream more loudly!

When you are planning your strategies you should remember that for a day or two at least, things could get worse. However, it can be most rewarding when a short time later, things start to get better and within six weeks you may well have forgotten there was a problem.

Some final thoughts

This book of ideas and suggestions is by no means complete. The aim has been to write a book long enough to be useful but not so long that you lose interest! A good book cannot replace good training and experience but it can be a useful prop and point of reference when difficulties arise.

The importance of 'joined-up working' (all professionals, parents and carers working together and keeping each other informed) cannot be stressed enough. Make sure information about what has happened in school and what is happening at home goes back and forth on a regular basis. This makes such a difference to the level of progress that is possible and can mean all kinds of damaging mistakes can be avoided.

Teachers, nursery officers and play leaders must work hard to get to know the children with autistic spectrum disorders as well as they know the other children in their class or nursery. Support workers are often on the front line, working closely with the children every day, but they should be supported by teachers and other colleagues, not left feeling isolated.

Special educational needs co-ordinators (SENCOs) also play an important role in ensuring that targets are set, reviews are carried out on time, training is organised and awareness is raised generally throughout the school.

Other professionals – who may include clinical and educational psychologists, speech and language therapists, specialist teachers and occupational therapists – should ensure that they know who is involved with the child and what advice is being given by different people. All reports about the child should be sent to parents.

Working with children with autistic spectrum disorders is very rewarding. Keep at it!

References

Baron-Cohen, S. (1995) *Mindblindness*, Cambridge, Massachusetts: MIT Press.

Baron-Cohen, S., and Bolton, P. (1993) *Autism: The Facts*, Oxford: Oxford University Press.*

Beyer, J., and Gammeltoft, L. (2000) *Autism and Play*, London: Jessica Kingsley.*

Goldbart, J. (1988) 'Re-examining the Development of Early Communication' in J. Coupe and J. Goldbart (eds) *Communication Before Speech: Normal development and impaired communication*, Beckenham, Kent: Croom Helm.

Gray, C. (1997) *Social Stories* and *Comic Strip Conversations*, Social Stories Unlimited Presentations and Workshops, Arlington, Texas: Future Horizons (available in the UK from Winslow).

Grandin, T. (1995) *Thinking in Pictures and other Reports from my Life with Autism*, New York: Vintage Books.*

Jordan, R., and Jones, G. (1999) *Meeting the Needs of Children with Autistic Spectrum Disorders*, London: David Fulton.*

Newman, S. (1999) *Small Steps Forward*, London: Jessica Kingsley.*

Newton, C. and Wilson, D. (1999) *Circles of Friends*, Dunstable: Folens Ltd.

Sussman, F. (1999) *More than Words*, Ontario: The Hanen Centre.

* Available from NAS Publications. For more information telephone 020 7903 3595

The National Autistic Society EarlyBird Programme
EarlyBird Centre, 3 Victoria Crescent West
Barnsley, South Yorkshire S75 2AE

Tel 01226 779218 Fax 01226 771014

Division TEACCH (Treatment and Education of Autistic and related Communication Handicapped Children), Administration and Research
CB 7180, 310 Medical School Wing E
University of North Carolina at Chapel Hill, Chapel Hill, North Carolina 27599-7180 USA

Tel +001 (919) 966 2173

For more information about TEACCH, contact the NAS Information Centre (tel 020 7903 3599) for a factsheet or visit the NAS website (www.nas.org.uk) and select the factsheet from the site index.

Further reading

Attwood, T. (1997) *Asperger Syndrome: A guide for parents and professionals*, London: Jessica Kingsley.*

Berger, A., and Gross, J. (1999) *Teaching the Literacy Hour in an Inclusive Classroom*, London: David Fulton.

Berger, A., Henderson, J., and Morris, D. (1999) *Implementing the Literacy Hour for Pupils with Learning Difficulties*, London: David Fulton.

Cumine, V., Leach, J., and Stevenson, G. (1997) *Asperger Syndrome: A practical guide for teachers*, London: David Fulton.*

Detheridge, T., and Detheridge, M. (1997) *Literacy Through Symbols: Improving access for children and adults*, London: David Fulton.

Gillingham, G. (1995) *Autism, Handle with Care*, Arlington, Texas: Future Horizons.

Gray, C. (1993) *The Original Social Story Book*, Arlington, Texas: Future Horizons (available in the UK from Winslow, Chesterfield, Derbyshire).

Jenison Public Schools, Jenison, Michigan (1994) *The New Social Story Book*, Arlington, Texas: Future Horizons (available in the UK from Winslow, Chesterfield, Derbyshire).

Lear, R. (1996) *Play Helps*, Oxford: Butterworth Heinemann.

Leicester City Council and Leicestershire County Council (1998) *Asperger Syndrome – Practical Strategies for the Classroom: A teacher's guide*, London: The National Autistic Society.*

Leicestershire County Council and Fosse Health Trust (1998) *Autism: How to help your young child*, London: The National Autistic Society.*

Lynch, C., and Cooper, J. (1991) *Early Communication Skills*, Bicester, Oxfordshire: Winslow Press (new edition available in the UK from Winslow, Chesterfield, Derbyshire).

Powell, S., and Jordan, R. (1997) *Autism and Learning: A guide to good practice*, London: David Fulton.*

Williams, D. (1996) *Autism: An inside-out approach*, London: Jessica Kingsley.

* Available from NAS Publications. For more information telephone 020 7903 3595

Useful resources

Pocket Colour Cards

Pocket-sized sets of language flashcards, including early objects, actions, sequences and opposites. An excellent resource for developing language skills. (Available from Speechmark Publishing Ltd, Telford Road, Bicester, Oxon OX26 4LQ; tel 01869 244 644; website: www.speechmark.net)

Colour Cards: Emotions

Clear photographs showing different emotions. Could be used to help develop an understanding of different emotions, build an awareness of facial expressions and what they mean. They can also be used to encourage children to develop a story by thinking about what is happening in the picture and what happened before and after. (Available from Speechmark Publishing Ltd, Telford Road, Bicester, Oxon OX26 4LQ; tel 01869 244 644; website: www.speechmark.net)

Colour Cards: Basic Sequences

These photo cards show simple, three-step sequences of routine events to help develop language and sequencing skills. (Available from Speechmark Publishing Ltd, Telford Road, Bicester, Oxon OX26 4LQ; tel 01869 244 644; website: www.speechmark.net)

300 Three-minute Games, by Jackie Silberg

Short games and songs for young children that help build adult/child relationships, develop language, listening, co-ordination, social interaction and early learning skills. (Available from Winslow, Goyt Side Road, Chesterfield, Derbyshire S40 2PH; tel 0845 921 1777)

Tell About It

A set of 26 picture stories designed to encourage children to sequence, predict and tell a story. Each sequence has four, five, six or seven cards. (Available from LDA, Duke Street, Wisbech, Cambridgeshire PE13 2AE; tel 01945 463 441; website: www: instructionalfair.co.uk)

Why? Because

Each pair of picture cards depicts a situation that can be used to sequence, predict what happens next, what happened before and as the starting point to develop a simple story. (Available from LDA, address details above)

Writing with Symbols 2000 (CD-ROM for PC)

Developing communication, language and literacy with pictures, symbols and words. This software includes symbols from the Rebus symbols collection and the Picture Communication Symbols developed by Mayer-Johnson Co. (Developed by Widgit Software Ltd, 26 Queen Street, Cubbington, Leamington Spa CV32 7NA; tel 01926 885 303; website: www.widgit.com)

Index